About the Author

Francis Bailey and his younger brother Oliver had an unusual upbringing on an urban farm. They both went to a public school at King Williams College in the Isle of Man. Francis went on to have an interesting career in banking, the motor and caravan trades and even paper making. His interest in all things technical eventually led to him settling down to work in local government as an IT manager for many years. He is now retired and lives in Nottingham.

Dedication

Bob and Nan, who were always there

Francis Bailey
with
Oliver Bailey

CORNFLAKES, PIGS AND A VULTURE CALLED SQUASHY

AUSTIN MACAULEY PUBLISHERS™

LONDON • CAMBRIDGE • NEW YORK • SHARJAH

A CIP catalogue record for this title is available from the British Library.

ISBN 9781787103900 (Paperback)
ISBN 9781787103917 (Hardback)
ISBN 9781787103924 (Kindle e-Book)
ISBN 9781528952460 (Epub e-Book)
www.austinmacauley.com

First Published (2019)
Austin Macauley Publishers Ltd
25 Canada Square
Canary Wharf
London
E14 5LQ

Acknowledgements

Thanks are due to those members of the family who have contributed to this entertainment. My sisters Susan and Linda, my sister in law Nan and my nephew Paul. They have reminded me of stories and corrected my failing memory. My cousin Margaret Rushton also kindly lent me the photograph of her jumping her horse at Didsbury Show and added the odd anecdote.

Thanks are due most especially to my brother Oliver. He is keeper of the family genealogy and history and also took part in many of the exploits in this book. I could not have done it without him.

Thanks are also due to the Manchester historian Andrew Simpson who has allowed me to plunder his historical blog of Chorlton for photographs and bits of history. I have also dragooned people into reading the various drafts and improving the content, punctuation and grammar so thanks are due to Dave Webb, Dave Singleton and my son-in-law Robin Docksey

Special thanks are due to my wife Vicky for her patience while I've battled with writing this. Her patience has been monumental, and this book would have been impossible without her help and encouragement.

I'd also like to thank Giselle Caruana for drawing and inspiring the cartoons that are scattered throughout the book to illustrate events that couldn't be photographed.

Finally, I'd like to mention Private Eye magazine for an article they ran in April 1971 about my dad. The details of that article can be found in Chapter 12.

Preface

This book came about as a result of the death of my older brother Bob in June 2015. My younger brother Oliver and I were asked by Bob's wife Nan to read eulogies at his funeral. So, we both independently decided to tell something of what life was like growing up with Bob and naturally, being three lively boys, there were plenty of daft incidents to choose from.

After the funeral, my son-in-law Robin asked if what we had told in church really happened or were we exaggerating a bit. I told him we weren't and that these were just a few of things that happened. And so, he said: "You mustn't leave it there. I've never heard of any of this stuff and most children don't grow up with those sort of things happening. Write it all down so the children and grand-children will know what life was like growing up in your family 60 – 70 years ago."

So here it is. Possibly a bit rose-tinted but that's to be expected as we all tend to remember the good stuff and, of course, it never rained when we were kids.

Francis Bailey
May 2017

Photo Credits

Most photos used are from the personal collections of my family and myself.

Exceptions are:

Photo of the Stone 'Beast' from the collection of Tony Walker and photo of the front of the Farm in the early 1970s from the Lloyd Collection. Both of these by courtesy of Manchester local historian Andrew Simpson.

The photo of Kellogg's factory in the 1950s and the one of Hough End Hall with Bonnie the Suffolk Punch are both courtesy of Manchester City Council Local Image Collection. With thanks to Jane Parr.

The photo of the Bristol 405 is courtesy of Geoffrey Herdman of the Bristol Owners Club.

Chapter One
And in the Beginning

It was all Granddad's fault.

I suppose that lots of us can say that because Granddads must do things that echo down the generations. So, we find ourselves living in places where we wouldn't have been if Grandad hadn't changed his job or just moved or whatever.

Anyway, in my case I know it was Granddad's fault, despite the fact that he died before I was born, because as a result of his death, my Dad didn't go where he was planning to go. And so, I was born in England and not Kenya. So, we possibly escaped being skewered by the Mau Mau in the 1950s.

To explain a little, my family's background was as small holders and latterly farmers living around Chorlton-cum-Hardy in South Manchester having arrived there in the early 1800s. In the 19th and early 20th centuries, Chorlton-cum-Hardy and nearby Stretford were little villages surrounded by fields worked by small-holders who sold their produce to feed the growing population of Manchester. By the 1920s, Granddad, Edmund Seymour Bailey, was living and working a small farm in what was by now a well-developed suburb/dormitory for Manchester, but Park Brow Farm, the farm he was renting from the Egerton Estate didn't have very much land for him to earn a crust from.

He and Grandma had eight children, seven boys and one girl. Two of the boys (Edmund and Harry) and the girl Elizabeth died very young, so it was five of the boys who grew up to manhood. One, Leonard was my father and the other four, William, Norman, Seymour and Eric were the uncles that I knew. William and Norman fought in the First World War, but the other three boys were too young. There's a brilliant photograph below taken in 1916 of Granddad and Grandma and their five boys with the two oldest boys wearing their army uniforms. Miraculously, Will and Norman survived the horrors of that War and came home to start a farm and a coal merchant's business respectively. The other brothers used to tease Norman that he'd only taken up the coal business because he'd been captured by the Germans and put to work down a coal mine while he was a PoW.

The five Brothers with Grandma and Grandpa Bailey.

L to R: Seymour, Norman, Eric, Will, Leonard (my Father)

By the mid-1920s, Dad wasn't married but was getting itchy feet and took up an offer to go to Kenya to work on a coffee plantation for local landowner, Lord Egerton. However, when Granddad died in 1925, Dad stayed on at Chorlton to help Grandma run the farm. The job on the coffee plantation had first been offered to my Uncle Seymour but he had just got engaged and so turned it down and the job was then offered to Dad instead. When Dad turned him down as well, Lord Egerton must have been pretty brassed off with indecisive Bailey boys.

Dad married Dora in 1930 and they lived in the old part of Chorlton in a house on Claude Road. My older sisters Linda and Susan were born there in 1931 and 1933 respectively. Then

Grandma decided to move out of the farm at the beginning of 1935 to live with my Uncle Norman whose coal merchants business was now established. So, Dad, Mum, Linda and Susan moved in to the farm in February and my older brother Bob was born there that April. Grandma died in 1936 and Dad carried on working the Farm. I arrived in 1942 and my younger brother Oliver arrived in 1943.

Dad had to provide for us all by making a living from a very small farm whose main source of income was a small herd of dairy cows that provided the milk for our local milk round plus some pigs. The milk round was very fragmented and unprofitable and one of the things they counted on for the budget was the rent Uncle Norman paid to keep his horses on our land. Had Dad been able to hang on until the start of the war, the milk round would have been OK as then milk rounds were consolidated and allocated by block.

But in the late 1930s something happened that was to change all that.

Chapter Two
The Coming of Kellogg's

In the USA, Cornflakes were making millions of dollars for W K Kellogg and his successors, but they fancied that they could make even more by setting up a plant in Europe. So, in 1938 they did just that and chose Trafford Park on the edge of Manchester for the location. Their big 1930s style factory is still there.

Their timing was rubbish because the Second World War was about to break out, but they got started and were producing cereals during the war and even produced some special cereals that used only British grown wheat. They were lucky not to get their factory bombed flat because Trafford Park was a major industrial centre and the Luftwaffe marked out the area for special attention.

Like all manufacturers, they produce waste and they advertised for people and companies to help with the waste disposal. Dad decided to answer the advert to see what was wanted because he had an area in one of his fields that sloped down towards a brook and was generally marshy and not good for anything. He felt that he might be able to use it as a tip site to take the Kellogg's waste – whatever it was.

He had a meeting with the people who were setting up the factory and found that they'd got two sorts of waste to get rid of. Firstly, they'd got spoilt packages and spillage. So that was mostly cardboard boxes that had come unglued or just gone wrong as they went into the packing machines. Mixed up with this were sweepings from spillage such as Corn Flakes and raw maize and wheat that had spilled. All of this would be OK to go down the marshy tip as it would all decompose in a year or so.

He got a big surprise though when they mentioned malting waste. Apparently, they were making their own malt which they used to flavour the cornflakes. Now Dad knew a bit about this because breweries had been making malt for centuries from barley and extracting the malt to flavour their beers. After they'd got the malt, the remaining mixture of barley grains and water made a very good animal food known as Brewers Grains. Kellogg's would be turning out exactly the same by-product, so Dad reckoned he could use this to feed his own cattle and pigs and probably sell on any surplus to local farmers.

At this stage, the factory wasn't in production and they were running through trial batches to get the equipment operating properly. At the same time, the British staff were being trained by people from the USA and Canada. Dad and the manager from the USA, a Mr Harry McEvoy, hit it off immediately and he also got on very well with Les Short from Toronto who was the Chief Engineer. They agreed to give Dad a trial while they were working up to production status and Dad started taking waste from the factory in a trailer towed behind the family car. McEvoy, who was usually called Mac, had a volcanic temper and when he was really going at it, Les Short would ring up Dad and say "Len - can you come in and talk to Mac for a bit. He's really got it on him today and he's giving everyone seven sorts of hell". Dad would turn up and Mac's innate politeness would stop him bellowing at Dad and then he'd start to chat to him and slowly calm down and peace would break out.

Les Short on the other hand, was very calm and even tempered. He was a big guy and seemed totally unflappable. Les and his wife Ethel, who was very petite, became very good friends of Dad and Mum and often visited the farm and even went on holidays with them. On one memorable occasion many years later, the Shorts were holidaying with Dad and Mum in the west of Ireland. Unbeknownst to them, my brother Oliver had been transferred by his company to Northern Ireland but had not been working there for very long. He'd also started to lose his hair so had compensated by growing a beard. Oliver found out the hotel they were staying in and decided to surprise them by going across there. Oliver was sat in the bar having a drink when Dad and Les Short came in. Oliver smiled at them and wished them a good evening, but Dad just glanced at him and carried on clearly thinking "*Bearded Weirdie*". Les Short on the other hand did a double take and said, "It isn't?" Oliver nodded and Les Short grinned, tapped Dad on the shoulder and said "Len. You've just walked past your own son!"

When the Shorts retired back to Toronto, they kept in touch and visited us on their trips to the UK. Dad and Mum returned the compliment and stayed with them in Canada. After they retired to Canada, the Shorts sent us a weekly bundle of newspapers, these being the weekend supplement of the Toronto Star that was called the Star Weekly. This was well before the days of Sunday supplements in UK newspapers and we were astonished at the amount of "free" reading matter they were giving out as travel, life style, serialised books, comics etc. We really enjoyed the comic section as it was full of exotic comic strips that were quite alien to Britain. About the only one that was familiar was '*Popeye*' but entirely new were *Dick Tracey, Li'l Abner, Steve Canyon, Blondie, Mandrake the Magician, Little Orphan Annie* etc. We loved them. When the musical Li'l Abner was released, and it bombed in the UK, we must have been one of the few UK families who 'got' what it was all about.

Kellogg's had by now realised that there was some value in the Grains from the malting room but didn't want to get into the business of supplying local farmers. They just wanted the stuff off site so that they could get on with producing breakfast cereals. So, a deal was done that noted that the grains had value, but Dad could take them away for free and his payment for getting them off-site would come from local farmers. The general waste was subject of a separate contract for which Dad got paid.

There was a sting in the tail of the contracts that said that Dad had to keep the factory clear so that a build-up of either grains or rubbish didn't interfere with the production of Corn Flakes. This was a canny move that recognised that Dad was just a small local businessman and might not be able to shift everything when the factory was running a full stretch. The family found out years later just what that sting meant when it came to keeping the factory clear of Grains in the middle of the night! We were only too aware that the contracts could be cancelled and bigger players brought in. Once Dad got going however, he became confident enough to go out and buy a small lorry though this was a year or two later.

Meanwhile, Dad got into talks with the Kellogg's management to decide how the waste and grains would be stored ready for him to collect. For the waste, it was simply a raised area with side walls that Dad's trailer or lorry could pull up alongside and it could all be shovelled in. The Grains were a different matter.

When the malting process was finished, the malting floor would be washed down, and the grains and water would drop into a tank, but this was inside the factory and a lorry couldn't get to it. So what Dad and Les Short schemed up was a hopper raised on legs that a lorry could back underneath, and this was to be at one side of the site so that our lorries weren't getting in the way of other vehicles delivering and collecting. The hopper would have a shutter that closed off the conical section at its base and this could be drawn back using a large hand wheel and screw thread. The grains would be moved out of the main factory building and into the hopper using a long pipe with a screw auger inside it. Then it was just a job of us backing a lorry underneath the hopper, turning the hand wheel and letting the Grains run into the lorry until it was full, when the shutter was closed.

Kellogg's Factory on Barton Dock Road in the 1950s

Now all this was happening in the late 1930s before I was born, but the family had got into the groove with the business. So, by the time I was old enough to really appreciate what was happening, the best part of 10 years had passed. Grains were going out to local farmers and rubbish was still being tipped on our bit of marshy ground that was naturally known to us boys as 'The Tip'. The difference, that I was blissfully unaware of, was that the family were now comfortably off and could afford to send all of the children to private schools. The two older girls were already at a local girls grammar school and my parents assumed that all three of us boys would eventually go on to boarding schools. Bob was sent a boarding grammar school near Preston and Oliver and I were told that we would take the so-called Common Entrance exam. This meant that we wouldn't move out of our primary school until the age of thirteen rather than eleven. So, we'd have quite a long stint at Moor Allerton, our primary school. To get to Moor Allerton School, which was a couple of miles away, we went on the bus, though instead of coming back on it, we regularly walked home and kept the bus fare that we'd saved. We were told that we might be saving bus fares, but we were wearing out our shoes quicker! This argument didn't convince Oliver and me because we didn't have to pay for shoe repairs!

Because of the big age difference, Oliver and I didn't have a lot to do with Linda and Susan except when we were very small, and they were helping Mum out by minding us and taking us for walks. We were both walked to and from our infant school which was just under a mile away by Mum or Linda or Susan if they were available until the age of seven. When we were a bit older, Susan used to take us walking in the Peak District. around Hope and Edale and once on a short walking holiday in the Lake District. So, we were both very used to walking everywhere but the farm was very much the centre of our universe.

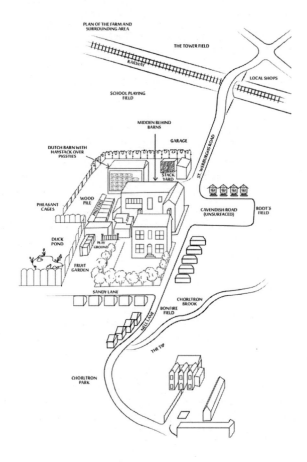

Chapter Three
The Farm

Park Brow Farm was located in the pleasant Manchester suburb of Chorlton-cum-Hardy and was right at the junction of two quiet roads. St Werburghs Road ran north away from the farm and then up and over a railway bridge after which it entered the suburbs properly and there was a small rake of local shops about quarter of a mile away. The other road was Sandy Lane which ended at a T junction with St Werburghs Road and two sides of our garden ran out to the T. Sandy Lane going the opposite way ran down towards Chorlton proper and it was fully built up with houses all the way from its junction with St Werburghs Road. The latter was less built up with just the farm and a small school playing field on the left-hand side before it reached the railway line and its bridge. The opposite side of St Werbughs Road from the farm had just a few houses on it, three pairs of big semi's and a couple of detached house. There was also a bit of land given over to a tennis club that was right beside the railway tracks. Right opposite the farm entrance was a little stub of a road named Cavendish Road that stopped short at the entrance to one of our fields known as Rootes Field. This little stub had just two pairs of semi's on one side of it and, although a properly named and adopted road, it wasn't properly surfaced with tarmac and was instead covered with rolled ash. Great for doing skids on our bikes! Rootes field got its name because it was leased to the car makers, Rootes Group, as their sports field.

The farm was about 180 years old so built in a pleasing Georgian style and all the buildings were a nice warm red brick though the lower parts of the barns had been whitewashed. The centre of the farm, in fact the centre of most farms, is the Yard.

You turned off the road and you were onto a cobbled slope that led you down into the yard with the farmhouse running alongside you on the left. Two other sides of the Yard were occupied by two storey farm buildings and the third side, opposite as you went in, was a higgledy-piggledy collection of mostly single storey buildings. They comprised two or three old fashioned pigsties with a pigeon loft over them plus a strange little building roofed in corrugated iron with an iron chimney sticking out of it. That was the boiler house. These were all whitewashed. There was an old cast iron lion painted a bright red fixed to the front wall of the pigeon loft that caught the eye as did the large stone trough just in front with its old-fashioned village pump painted green.

Entrance to the Farm in the early1970s

The steps on the right of the entrance lead up to the Garner

That stone trough had its own special part in history when Paulo's circus was held in our field that we knew as the Tower Field in about 1940. People from the circus used to bring the two elephants, Salt and Saucy to water them at our trough. Brother Bob rode home from school on one of them to his great delight and envy of his mates. He was perched up on the back of Salt like a Rajah, though a Rajah in short pants and grubby knees. In later years Bob was given a book by his wife Nan that told the story of these two elephants who were quite famous in their time. We nearly became elephant owning farmers when Salt and Saucy were offered to Dad for the duration of the war as long as he fed them, but he declined as the buyback price wasn't guaranteed. I also wonder where on earth he would have kept them! Oliver and I weren't quite born so missed this early example of Dad's passion for animals.

The Yard itself was big enough to park three lorries of about 5-ton capacity and had an L shaped range of two storey buildings on the opposite side to the farmhouse. There were some external stone steps that led up to an upper storey store that was always known as the Garner and there was an opening under the steps so that the space there could be used as a dog kennel. The Garner wasn't really used for anything much and was unofficially a place that us three boys used. Bob had a large train layout up there. As small boys, Oliver and I had the run of the farm when we were not at school and both Dad and Mum had a very relaxed view of what we got up to. However, we were told not to mess with Bob's stuff, especially his trains, while he was away. Bob was taking no chances however and kept the door to the Garner locked and we could only visit it when he was there. It wasn't until I was quite a bit older that I appreciated why he was very careful. I hadn't realised that he'd made all the track himself. He'd bought rails, chairs (the little brackets that hold the rails), sleepers and lengths of timber from Basset Lowke's shop in Manchester. Then he'd built straights, curves, points and cross-overs to create this large 0-gauge layout on which he ran live steam locomotives. In later years Bob kept a canoe up the Garner that he started building at school but brought home to finish. Oliver and I kept bikes up there and I last remember using it just before I got married to store the furniture that was being restored by me and my wife-to-be.

At ground level was the rambling workshop fitted out with benches and tools for fixing or making anything needed. The long leg of the L-shaped buildings at ground floor level contained the milking parlour, some pig cotes and a large area that had been used for stabling or keeping more cattle. Above these were a selection of lofts – an open fronted hay loft, a spare loft that was only used infrequently as a feed store, a pigeon loft and a two-level loft called the Chop Loft. You got up to the pigeon loft and the Chop loft by scrambling precariously up wall mounted wooden ladders but for the others, you had to drag out an ordinary ladder to get to them.

In a typical farmyard way, there was assorted livestock running about. There were plump brown Rhode Island Red chickens and scruffy looking Muscovy ducks waddling about. We used to rear some chickens for sale and keep some for laying. Bob taught Oliver and me how to hypnotise a chicken, which is the sort of life skill all young boys need. You caught your chicken then held it down with its beak close to the ground. Then you put a finger down in front of the chicken's beak and drew it slowly away from it for about 4 inches and repeated the process for about a minute. When you released the chicken, it would stay there completely mesmerised until you gave it a bit of a push whereupon it would wake up with a squawk and totter off.

The yard chickens came from fertile eggs that Dad had bought at the market and we'd keep them in an incubator, turning them every day. When the chicks hatched out, they were moved into the kitchen where they lived at the bottom of a cosy cupboard next to the fireplace. The Muscovy ducks roosted in the hay loft on the far side of the yard and flapped down from there. They would nest up there and when their ducklings were big enough, they'd assemble them on the edge of the loft looking down on the yard and encourage them to flutter down the 10 feet or so to the ground. There were also several geese strutting around that used to honk and hiss at us children until we were shown how to scare them off. Linda showed me that when a goose came at you hissing and flapping, instead of backing off you went forward making a hissing sound yourself and with your hand stretched out in front of you making a grabbing motion aimed at the goose's neck. They thought that they were going to be grabbed by the neck and so they backed off.

Another inhabitant, and the one-time, undisputed monarch of the farmyard, was Abdul, a large, very bad-tempered turkey cock. Except for Dad, everyone was frightened of Abdul who would strut about, gobbling away and puffing his feathers out to show how big and important he was. If he got near you, he'd give you a good pecking. He made a point of terrorising Mum until one day Dad decided that it was time for Abdul to be shown that he couldn't get away with this anymore. He got a big knobbly walking stick, gave it Mum and told her to go out in yard and, if Abdul went for her, she was to whack him one with the stick.

Abdul was parading round the yard in his best show-off style with tail up, wings down and a haughty tilt to his head.

Mum went out somewhat fearfully, clasping the stout walking stick while the family crowded into the doorway to watch.

Abdul saw her, gobbled fiercely and strode towards her.

Mum gave him a bit of a tap with the stick.

This clearly puzzled Abdul as he paused, shook his wattles and then came on.

This time Mum really whacked him one and he backed off.

Mum, now realising that she'd got the upper hand, went after Abdul and chased him round the yard, whacking him whenever she got within range.

Abdul gave up and ran away into the Stackyard and Mum proudly returned to the house to a hero's welcome.

The next day, Abdul was found dead. Drowned in one of the vats of pig swill. He was known to flutter up on to the swill vats and pick at the contents so perhaps he lost his footing and fell in. We thought it more likely that he'd jumped in and drowned himself in shame at being humiliated by Mum.

There was one other odd thing in the yard, and this was a
strange D-shaped structure just underneath one of the windows
of the house. It was about 5 feet long and protruded 3 feet into
the Yard. It was surrounded by a 2 feet high stone parapet with
a hefty wooden lid on top. With the lid off, you could see that it
led down to the cellar under the house so was probably put in
when the house was first built for things to be delivered direct
to the cellar or it might have been to let light in. We always
knew it as 'The Escape Hatch'. This was because during the
Second World War, our house being one of the few with a cellar
was nominated as an Air Raid Shelter. Apparently, all the
neighbours took shelter in our cellar whenever there was an air
raid and it was fitted out with bunks to park all the children on
and deck chairs for the adults. It must have been a heck of a
crush because it wasn't a very big cellar. It was intended that if
the house got bombed and people couldn't get out of the cellar
via the stairs, then they could escape up the old coal chute.
Hence 'The Escape Hatch'. Manchester, and especially the
Trafford Park Industrial were regularly targeted for air raids and
the house did get hit twice by incendiaries during the raids.
Happily, Dad and the neighbours managed to put them out

though after the war, some ceiling joists that had been weakened by the bombs gave way and deposited the ceiling into our boys bedroom There was another near miss when two good sized bombs hit the field about 250 yards away, very close to Hough End Hall, and the hole left in the field was known to all as Bomb Crater Corner. The blast from these blew Dad over when he was out that night on Fire Watch.

The farm house made very little impression on the first-time visitor as it was sideways on to the Yard entrance and this was its rear aspect. So, you walked into the yard and almost as an afterthought said "Oh. There's the farmhouse. And which of the two green painted back doors is the right one to knock at?" That became clear when you spotted the bell push by the far door. The first door was fixed shut for as long as I can remember and had a chest of drawers wedged up against the inside of it with the parrot's cage on top containing a handsome African Grey parrot who was quite chatty but who liked to spread the husks from his sunflower seeds and peanuts as far around as possible.

The other side of the farmhouse faced the garden. Being a Georgian building, the front elevation looked like every child's drawing of a house. Front door in the centre, four nice square small paned windows evenly spread across the front and a small single window directly above the front door. As you stood in front of the house with your back to the door, the garden was ahead of you and, further to your right and separated from the main garden by a long run of rhododendrons, was the fruit and vegetable garden. Finally, and completely to your right was another grassed area where Mum had her clothes lines and where we used to play. Always known as the Playground it was dominated by three very large Sycamore trees that defined the boundary between garden and playground.

The garden was Dad's pride and joy and it looked beautiful at any time of the year. I can just remember the garden as it was in war-time with almost all of it given over to vegetable production and with bee hives up one side to provide the sweeteners that were otherwise unavailable during the war. However, in the late 1940s Dad set about making it a proper garden. He built a nice York stone terrace in front of the house and then built a low stone wall along the edge of the new terrace to separate it from the lawn-to-be. The wall had a planted space in the top which was planted with sedums and alpines and had two pillars about 3 feet high that marked the steps leading down to the lawn. The garden was about 100 feet long to where it terminated at Sandy Lane. Its left-hand edge was separated from the side of St Werburghs Road and the first bit of Sandy Lane by a large L-shaped privet hedge about 7 feet tall that gave us privacy. Just inside the privet hedge was a long border that ran round the large lawn and was planted with perennials and annuals that provided stunning colours throughout the year. Dotted among the flowers were about six crab apple trees that provided beautiful blossom in the spring plus a fine crop of crab apples in the autumn from which Mum made excellent crab apple jelly. There were a couple more good size trees in the bed at the end of the lawn, a Pine tree that was a lovely bluey green colour (possibly a Cedrus Atlanticus) and a rather rare Ginkgo and a Japanese Flowering Cherry half way down the lawn on the right. It was a very attractive garden and Dad was justifiably proud of it.

The big lawn dominated the view and was kept in trim with a crotchety ATCO 2-stroke motor mower. Once you'd got it started, it was fine, but it was always reluctant to spring into life. So once started, you left it running even when you had to leave it to empty the grass box. This you did with fingers crossed that it wouldn't stop while you were missing or worse, vibrate itself into gear and set off on its own making a mess of the nice even stripes you were trying to create.

Down the right-hand side of the lawn ran a very narrow rose bed and beside that was a path surfaced in crushed stone that ran all the way from the Yard and up to the Sandy Lane end of the garden. Under this path was buried the main water supply to the farm house and in the savage winter of 1947, the whole length of pipe froze solid. This was obviously a big problem for the house but fortunately, the farm supply was separate and didn't freeze. All the able-bodied men set to digging out the length of the pipe back to the stop cock beside Sandy Lane and then set about gently thawing it with blowlamps hoping to avoid a burst but failing regularly. It was a long job. Once we'd got running water restored, the men dug the trench for the pipe out to another 18inches lower and re-set

26

the pipe at the lower level it was hoped that frost couldn't reach.

In the area behind the Yard was a roadway leading round to a second yard where stood a large Dutch barn and the vast smelly midden where all the pig and cow muck was dumped. This area was always known as the Stackyard and it had a separate entrance off the road. There was also a rather tumbledown collection of sheds covered in corrugated iron that was rented out as a garage business to a family called Booth and the Booths accessed their area by this second entrance. There were other bits of the farm scattered about including pigsties, a duck pond and wood yard and the whole lot occupied an area of 2-3 acres.

The wood yard deserves a bit of explanation. Dad used to buy 'chippings' from a local timber merchant called Parkers of Ancoats. Chippings are the little chips of wood that fly off when timber goes through a planing machine and Parkers had tons of the stuff. We used to buy whole lorry loads of the stuff because it made it a superb bedding material for the pigs. It was light, easily spread and very absorbent. It was a bit like permanent snowflakes. It also rotted down very well in the midden (muck heap to us) when we cleaned out the pig sties. Parkers used to turn up with one of those wonderful Scammel three wheeled tractor units pulling a big trailer which they parked up in the Yard outside the building that we used as a chipping store. Then farm hands, kids and friends would get stuck in to shovel the chippings into the store. It was light work, it smelt wonderful as only freshly cut timber can, and we all got covered with the stuff as the chippings stuck to clothing and hair. But you didn't want them in your eyes as they were scratchy. After we'd done shovelling, everyone stood in the yard while we got swept down and then checked for cleanliness by Mum before we were allowed back in the house. She would wail: "What will their parents think!" as our friends left to go home with bits of chippings still stuck to them.

The Scammel would turn up later to collect the empty trailer and sometimes brought another one with a load of timber off cuts in it. These were usually shortish broken lengths of machined timber or sometimes unfinished lengths of planking. This all got dumped in the wood yard in a great heap and were used for kindling for the farmhouse's coal fires or fuel for the stove in the hut the farm hands used. For some reason, this latter was called the Shant. Strange word. Maybe an abbreviation of shanty. About this time Dad bought a circular saw with a 3-foot blade that he used to cut the stuff up into useful lengths. He quickly changed the push button starter switch to something more secure to stop us kids doing something stupid – as if we would! As it happens, we were all very cautious around that circular saw because of what had happened to Dad. He'd lost two fingers off his right hand to a circular saw many years before and that was an awful warning to us kids.

We children loved poking around in the wood pile trying to find useful bits than we could make dens out of. A popular game was playing Toss the Caber when suitably long bits were hoisted into the air to try to get them over the other side of the wood pile. Ideally while scaring whoever was on the other side without actually injuring them.

To this day, whenever I see the word "Pal" in a book or magazine, I automatically think of Parkers the timber merchants. This is because "Parkers Ancoats Limited" was abbreviated to PAL and painted in large letters on their smart, dark blue Scammels as well as the full name. The other day, I was watching an edition of the '*Salvage Squad*' TV programme in which they'd restored a Scammel tractor unit. It was still impressive to see the tractor unit turn in its own length and automatically connect up to different trailers with just the driver doing it. Clever stuff for the 1930s/40s.

This was how I remember the main part of farm from the late 1940s and it changed slowly over the years. There were just the few fields close by and also Hough End Hall and farm that we rented about quarter of a mile away.

Chapter Four
Hough End Hall

Hough End Hall and its farm was also owned by Lord Egerton's estate but rented out to our family. It was about quarter of a mile away along St Werburghs Road but in the opposite direction from the railway. However, St Werburghs Road changes its name to Nell Lane after its junction with Sandy Lane, so it was Nell Lane that dipped down and up again as it crossed Chorlton Brook and carried on past Hough End on its way towards Didsbury. Our fields were on the left-hand side of Nell Lane while Chorlton Park was on the right, so it was a pleasant walk to get to Hough End with just a few houses on the right as Nell Lane began.

When we were small children, the fields at Hough End sloped gently down towards the brook and part of this was the area used by my father for tipping the waste from Kellogg's. The word "brook" conjures up images of a tinkling stream, its dappled waters splashing over boulders with minnows darting about amongst its reed-sprinkled margins. Think again! The reality of Chorlton Brook in the 1940's and 50's was that it was a heavily polluted mini river that took drainage water from a wide area. Its waters were distinctly murky and full of strange growths of algae that hung in tattered banners from odd branches that had washed down and got themselves jammed in the banks or the bed. We were strictly forbidden to play in or near it. The ban was reinforced by warnings about Jinny Greenteeth. This was a mythical fishy monster with shark-like teeth that lurked in the depths of the brook just waiting to sink its teeth into the tender flesh of innocent children who strayed near its lair. We kept well away. For a few years anyway.

The tipping field, or simply 'Tip' as we came to call it was one of only two fields that made up Hough End Hall and its farm and they both had Chorlton Brook to define their limit. There was no farm house. Just the hall and a collection of farm buildings in a sort of T shape. There was a yard with a duck pond enclosed on one side by the Hall and its garden, on two more sides by the leg and one arm of the T, and on the fourth side was a wall separating the yard from the field that became the Tip. On the other side of the leg of the T was a small muddy field that was hemmed in by roads and was usually a total mud bath from the pigs that grubbed about in it.

Hough End Hall itself was a genuine medieval manor house and was probably built at the end of the 16th century. It had a very imposing frontage and the inevitable myth that Queen Elizabeth I had stayed there. It looked a lot like the sort of places that she actually <u>did</u> stay in but I'm sure she didn't because it was quite small and actually only a couple of rooms deep. Father let out the hall to a succession of tenants one of whom was an elderly family named Wood. It can't have been very convenient to live in as there was only a bare minimum of a kitchen and bathroom but, in the immediate post war years, people took whatever kind of roof over their heads that they could get. I don't think it even had hot water. But it did have a Haunted Room as we discovered some years later.

The Wood's seemed to regard the Hall and all the associated buildings as their private fiefdom and used to chase us kids off the farmyard when we sometimes went up there to play. This of course rebounded on them as we soon learnt to bait them. We'd go up to Hough End and start playing in full view of the hall, probably with homemade boats on the duck pond but keeping an eye out for the Woods. Once the front door of the hall opened, we'd scarper and hide either behind a wall or around the corner of a building. One of the Woods, usually the wife, would stand at the end of the garden shouting imprecations. Then she'd go inside. We'd give it a few minutes for her to get comfortable and then go back and start playing again. Mrs Wood would come out again and we'd disappear only to start again once we'd given her a couple of minutes to get settled in her favourite chair. After three or four rounds of this, she'd give up and we'd continue to play triumphantly.

Naturally Mrs Wood complained to Father who had to remind her politely that she was only a tenant of the hall and, while it was kind of her to keep an eye on the place, the rest of the farm was quite open for his children to play in. Her scowls whenever we appeared told us that she was definitely not happy.

There were a couple of other tenants of the hall buildings who we used to go and visit. There was a working blacksmith's shop in one of the hall's outbuildings and we used to go and watch a man called John Hallsworth who had the blacksmith's shop in the 1950s. He had been a blacksmith with British Road Services and rented the smithy at Hough End from my father after he retired from British Road Services. He was into wrought iron – he made a couple of ornate gates for Park Brow Farm. But he didn't shoe horses. However, on one occasion, Sam & Jack Priday - who were farriers with a smithy in Withington - came round and used Hallsworth's forge to shoe Bonnie my father's Suffolk Punch horse. Oliver remembers walking beside him as he used a horse drawn single furrow plough in the field next to Mauldeth Road, probably in the late 1940s.

Bonnie the Suffolk Punch outside Hough End Hall. The little extension sticking out at the right of the picture is where John Hallsworth's forge was located

John Hallsworth was kept busy making wrought iron gates, fencing and fittings and he even made some steel pig cote doors for the farm. When we were there, it was always a treat to be allowed to work the massive bellows for the forge, though we had to stand on a box to reach the top handle of the bellows which was well above our heads. The other tenant at Hough End was a character named Jimmy Ryan. He rented loft space in one of the farm outbuildings and in there Jimmy bred rabbits. He'd inherited his first rabbits from Dad but now kept mostly fancy rabbits for show, but he never seemed to run out of loft space to keep them in, despite the prolific breeding habits of rabbits. We assume that the less photogenic ones were disappearing into the pot. Apart from enjoying looking at the exotic rabbits with big ears and big fur, we kept well in with

Jimmy because he worked at Metropolitan Vickers in Trafford Park. From the stores at Metrovick's he could acquire considerable quantities of small nuts and bolts which were just the right size to use in Meccano. For this, he was a popular character with all us boys.

The rest of the farm buildings at Hough End were mostly used by father to keep pigs. We kept a lot of pigs as you will read later. There was also a loft in which he experimented with keeping chickens in the "Deep Litter" method. If you were keeping chickens for their eggs before the war, there were basically two ways of going about it. You could keep them in open runs with a hen house in which they stayed at night and laid their eggs. The other way was in battery cages, intensive and cost effective but expensive to get started in. Deep Litter was the newer alternative in which the hens were kept in very large enclosed spaces with a deep layer of sawdust/wood shavings/straw on the floor and lit by lighting that was controlled by a timer. There were perches fitted all around and the chickens could lay their eggs anywhere. It required a daily visit to go round the whole space looking for and collecting the eggs which could take some time. The feeders had to be topped up every day, the lights and timers had to be checked but they had automatic watering points. Once a year, the chickens were sold off, all the litter on the floor, now full of chicken muck, had to be shovelled out and carted to the muck heap. The space was then fumigated, refilled with litter and a fresh batch of chickens installed. Next time you're buying free range eggs, they'll probably be from hens kept inside just like ours unless it says that the open air was involved somewhere on the box.

The Deep Litter process wasn't very labour efficient compared to battery cages. However, the chickens were supposedly less stressed compared to battery chickens and laid better, and almost as many eggs. Father kept it going for a number of years and then built a Battery House at Park Brow. After seeing the results, that was the end of Deep Litter at Hough End. And also, the end of one of my after-school tasks. I quite liked the egg collecting but I didn't enjoy tramping through the shitty litter nor removing the occasional dead chicken. There was also the problem that if it was a cold winter, the pipes would freeze and then we had to set to with a blowlamp to get the water flowing again to the automatic watering points. Then we had to repair the bursts. Foam lagging was a distant dream in those days.

After the last tenants left the hall, the place lay empty for a few years, so we finally got to go inside. Great fun. A spooky old Manor House to explore. Dad quite fancied the idea of living in a medieval hall but after one look, Mum was having none of it. It wasn't that big, and it wasn't in very good condition. In one of the upper rooms we found a mighty box mangle. For those who've never seen one, box mangles are impressive bits of kit and are believed to date to 17th or 18th centuries. There's a sturdy table about 30 inches high that's about 7 feet long and about 3 feet wide. Resting on this table are three or four wooden rollers that looked like very large rolling pins. Then sitting on top of the rollers was a deep box filled with stones. A contraption of ropes, pulleys and a hand wheel made the heavy box move backwards and forwards, rolling on the rollers. Sheets and tablecloths that needed to be pressed or smoothed were fed under the rollers by one of the servants while another worked the handle to roll the rollers across the top of them. What this massive brute of a machine was doing in a hall as small as Hough End is a mystery as they're usually to be found in only the biggest country houses. I know that there's one at Shugborough Hall in Staffordshire.

The Egerton family also owned Tatton Hall near Knutsford and this was their main home. They moved the staircase from Hough End to Tatton Hall and it's still there to this day. The Mighty Mangle would have been more suited to a house the size of Tatton so it's interesting to speculate that it could have come from there and the Egertons swapped a mangle for a staircase!

A Box Mangle

So, we rolled it backwards and forwards a few times to see how it worked and that was it. I think that Dad offered it to Manchester Museum, but they weren't very interested, and I remember that it had woodworm which they wouldn't want to spread to their more exotic items. Unlike today, Museums in the 1950's weren't really into collecting stuff that was part of everyday life and less than 300 years old unless it was something exciting. They might have exhibited Oliver Cromwell's helmet but not Oliver Cromwell's mangle. Doesn't have the same appeal does it? I've no idea what happened to the Mighty Mangle though Oliver thinks it may have gone to Ordsall Hall in Salford.

After a bit more exploring, we set off in search of the Haunted Room. All old houses have stories and rumours about ghosts and Hough End was no exception. Except in this case it was supposed to have a Haunted Room that may have been a Priest Hole so was hard to find. About four of us, all aged about ten were poking around, tapping walls and then upstairs we found a bit of painted panelling that sounded hollow when tapped. Looking at it closely, we worked out that it could be a door and with some poking and prying with pen knives, we prised it open. Immediately in front of were two or three steps that led up into a small chamber that had no windows or exit. Was this it? We shuffled inside, and one brave soul pulled the door to, so we were in total darkness. Now I don't believe in ghosts, spooks or spirits but what happened next, I've never forgotten. After a few moments I suddenly noticed that the temperature had dropped markedly. It got icy cold. Next thing is, I get a really unpleasant taste in my mouth. And I'm clearly not the only one as the four of us dashed down the few steps and out into the passage before rushing outside. I don't know what it was or how it happened, but I never went into that hidden room again. Or anywhere near it!

Chapter Five
Scavenging on The Tip

The Tip was in a use for a few years only and took the 'spoilt' waste from Kellogg's factory floor. This was cardboard packets, wax paper and loose Corn Flakes, Rice Krispies etc. It was mostly leftovers from accidents in the packaging process. I never knew why this waste stopped coming to us for tipping. It could have been because of more stringent licensing of tipping, better process control at Kellogg's or simply the fact that we'd tipped enough to fill in the boggy meadows sloping down to Chorlton Brook. I do know that furnace ash was tipped on top to bind it followed by topsoil and it was then allowed to green over. Looking at the part of the field now, sloping more steeply down to Brook than in the 1940s, you'd never guess that it had been used as tip. Or that it concealed hidden childhood treasures!

In the early 1950s, Kellogg's were promoting their cereals for children with giveaways. These took the form of things printed on the back of the cereal packets that you could cut out and play with. Animal or carnival masks were one favourite as were the cut-out figures of people with costumes you could fit on. For us, the time when Kellogg's really put it over on the opposition from Shredded Wheat and Weetabix was when they launched their Space Fleet. On the back of the cereal packets, they printed cut out space ships, launchers, ray guns and moon bases. And best of all, once you'd cut them out and stuck them together (with LePage's gum of course) many of them worked. You could cut out and glue a ray gun, fit it with an elastic band and then fire the streamlined cardboard missiles. The same thing went for the space ships that came in assorted shapes. You had to ballast the noses of them with paperclips (same as for the missiles) and then they would fly pretty well when launched from an elastic band powered launcher.

The snag for us kids was that you only got through one packet of cereal every couple of weeks, so it could take an agonisingly long time to build up your collection. Also, this was before the days of supermarkets, so you couldn't take each packet off the shelf looking for the one rocket or space station part that you really wanted. You had to take what the grocer handed you. Complaining that it was 'the wrong packet' would probably earn you a clip round the ear.

However, we were the kings of Cornflake Collectables. Lots of broken open cereal packets were being delivered several times a week to be dropped on the Tip. So, a-scavenging we would go armed with any garden tool we could smuggle away from the farm. Across St Werburghs Road, carry on down Nell Lane and the bridge over Chorlton Brook then on up the other side, through a hole in the fence and up onto the tip to start searching. With a bit of persistence, you could collect the whole set of twelve or so Space Fleet models in an hour or so. You'd discard three or four torn or trampled on packs for every good one, but they were there. No waiting for six months to collect them while your family crunched their way through their breakfasts. Other kids latched on to the fact that we'd got the set and wanted to know the secret, so we let trusted friends come round to play with us and then a few of us would slope off to the Tip and dig. It wasn't messy or smelly, just cardboard, wax paper and breakfast cereals under foot so mums and dads weren't complaining about the state that their kids were coming home in.

Then came the submarines. The US Navy ordered its first nuclear powered submarine – USS Nautilus – in the early 1950s. This was a 'Wow' moment for submarines as this was the first 'real' submarine that could stay submerged for days at a time. Kellogg's decided to celebrate the Nautilus by giving away plastic models of it in their Cornflake packets. The models were only about 2 inches long, but they worked! You removed a little plastic plug from the bottom of the sub, put a pinch of your mum's baking soda in the cavity revealed then put the plug back in. Then you put the sub in the bath or a bucket of water. It promptly sank slowly to the bottom but after about 10 seconds, it magically started to rise to the surface. Once on the surface, it slowly heeled over until it released a bubble of gas – this was CO_2 being generated by the action of water on the baking soda. Once the bubble had been released, the sub sank to the bottom and carried on the process until all the baking soda was used up. What a super little free toy. And these started turning up on the Tip as they came out of the broken packets. We soon had quite a fleet.

Experiments were conducted to see how long we could keep them going for. How deep they would go in the duck pond and how fast we could make them cycle using Andrews Liver Salts as racing fuel. The duck pond experiments led to a new sport. By this age Oliver and I had acquired air rifles. Pretty Mickey Mouse affairs with no real power, though a poorly aimed one would no doubt have taken an eye out. Submarine shooting contests were duly started. We'd fuel up half a dozen subs and throw them into the green and murky waters of the duck pond. Once they popped up, we'd try to hit them with air rifles. Our very own shooting gallery – with the real live ducks keeping well out of the way. No doubt when the duck pond was drained years later after the farm was sold, I'm sure the workmen must have been puzzled by the number of miniature plastic submarines that they dug out of the mud!

There was one other spin off from the Tip activities. We got less and less cardboard and wax paper being dropped off at the Tip because Kellogg's started to bale it up using a machine not unlike a farmer's hay baler. I don't know where the bales were being sent on a regular basis but there was less waste for Dad's lorries to bring to the Tip. However, every autumn several lorry loads of these wax paper/cardboard bales would be dropped off at the farm. These would be used to build a giant bonfire for Guy Fawkes Night by stacking them into a great heap supported by long chunks of timber making a wigwam shape in the centre. This was always held on a small field across the road and the whole neighbourhood would turn up so there would be over a hundred people there.

The bonfire was massive and incredibly hot, and we loved it because as well as the fireworks, all the neighbours brought trays of parkin and toffee that they passed around to everyone. When the fire had died down a bit, baked potatoes were cooked in the embers at the edge, being pushed in and pulled out with long stoker's scrapers as you couldn't get within 6 feet of the blaze until very late in the evening. Always a great night and a really good social event for the neighbourhood. The following day, we would be out early to search for all the fireworks that had been dropped or failed to go off and some years we would have about twenty or even thirty, bangers, roman candles, rockets, you name it. The ones that had failed to go off were always a bit dodgy if you tried to re-light them, so our favoured technique was to push them into the embers of the bonfire that was usually still glowing and let them cook until they went off. Thinking about it today, we were prime candidates to have become some of those awful Bonfire Night Accident statistics, but we somehow got away with it. As you'll have gathered, we always really looked forward to bonfire night – and the preceding weeks when we were letting off fireworks willy-nilly.

Chapter Six
Of Pigs – and Policemen!

Dad had kept pigs for as long as I could remember, and I believe that Grandpa did before him There were just three pigsties in the main yard at the farm and I suspect that they dated from Georgian times when the farm was built. Simple brick built outdoor runs with an undercover sleeping area behind, on top of which was a loft for pigeons. They were virtually the first things that you saw when you turned into the main Yard off the road, as well as the boiler house next to the pig cotes – of which, more later.

Dad built a long range of new pigsties behind the original three in the Yard plus a further four totally enclosed ones that were used for farrowing where the sows could give birth undisturbed. These four were kitted out with heaters that warmed the back part of each sty and this 3-foot rear section was separated from the main part of the sty by steel poles fixed into the brickwork. There were corrugated iron sheets bolted to the poles creating a strong barrier with a gap of about a foot between barrier and floor. The idea was that when a sow had given birth (farrowed), the piglets could get under the barrier into the nice warm area behind and weren't lying around to be squashed by the sow when she moved. A regular fate of slow-moving piglets before we had these special pens made.

I mentioned earlier that there was a large Dutch barn in the Stackyard at the rear of the farm. This was modified by Dad when he enclosed the lower part of it with brick to create three very large pigsties. These had big open runs at the front and enclosed sleeping areas covering about a third of the area of each sty. These enclosed areas were built with walls about 5 feet high compared to the 3-foot-high walls for the open areas.

The enclosed areas were then covered with a flat roof of stout timbers and hay and straw bales were then stacked on top. It made the pigs sleeping quarters nice and snug while the hay and straw was sheltered from the weather by still being under the roof of the barn.

This high-level hay stack was a great place to play and build dens, but you had to be careful not to move so many bales that the outside wall of your den was now the last row of bales. If it was, there was a good chance that if you fell against it while larking around, the whole wall, probably along with you, would topple into the pigsty on one side or the ground on the other. Either way, the drop was 5 feet from the bottom of the stack to the ground plus the height up the stack that your den had been built. I managed to fall out of both sides. The fall on the ground side I clearly remember as I sailed through the air clutching on to a bale of hay, landed with thud that shook the breath out me, then lay there terrified while bales came cascading down all around me. I kept quiet about that one for fear of being banned from playing in the hay stack. The fall off other side into the pig sty was just as dramatic but much bloodier as I landed on my head on the concrete floor of the pigsty and was recovered, pouring blood, by anxious parents. That was when we did get banned from playing up there until we were older.

In 1953 the hay stack caught fire – always believed to be the son of a neighbour smoking – but Oliver and I escaped suspicion as we were at a swimming lesson at the time. This was a very big deal and Sister Linda and Brother Bob charged into the pigs sleeping quarters with the stack blazing away above them. Incredibly brave of them and out of about a hundred pigs, only eleven died. There were even articles in the local newspapers "Brother and Sister defy flames to rescue Pigs." *News of the World,* I think. The fire brigade stayed for twenty-four hours apparently a requirement for that sort of fire in case bales of straw burst open and started to burn again. The Dutch barn was maybe 50ft high at the peak with a slate roof and with all the rafters partially burnt they decided they had to remove the slates to make it safe. This they did with great gusto using high pressure hoses to break them away from the fastenings and the slates were falling like giant grey snowflakes but landing with a satisfying smash.

Anyway, back to piggier business. Dad was fond of pigs and specialised in two breeds – Middle Whites with long snouts and placid Berkshires with their flattened ones. He was very successful at breeding and we had George as a special pig man who prepared the best of them for entry into Agricultural Shows. He had a large wooden chest in which he kept all his special stuff for shows. Soap, shampoo, brushes, oil and wood flour. Once he'd washed them, he got them shampooed, brushed until they were dry and then given a final oiling to polish them and the wood flour was rubbed in to make the Berkshires extra glossy. Dad and George were very successful and very proud of the fact that the inside lid of the wooden chest was smothered with rosettes the pigs had won. Firsts and Seconds, Champions and Best in Show. Thirds weren't really worth displaying. These prize rosettes were from shows all over the North West.

In later years, Dad bought just weaned young pigs and fattened them up to sell on for bacon. Fattening up weaners as they were called was less showy than breeding champion porkers but a lot less trouble and almost as profitable. The weaners were usually delivered by livestock truck and there would be a hugely entertaining half hour while these highly excitable young pigs were persuaded to come out of the truck in reasonable sized batches and then be guided to the sties we wanted them in by family and farmhands using sheets of corrugated iron and sticks. Pigs were squealing, men were yelling and dogs barking. Inevitably some made a break for it and there would be a mad dash to shut the yard gates to stop them getting out onto the road before setting off in pursuit and chasing the runaways all around the farm. Catching them was best achieved by grabbing a back leg and heaving them in the air so that they couldn't get much traction with their front legs then getting help to complete the capture. They were surprisingly muscular little blighters.

In the 1940s, we also sometimes got deliveries of young pigs by rail to the goods yard of Chorlton-cum-Hardy station. This was just over half a mile away. We didn't have a livestock truck, so we'd organise a Pig Drive and herd them through the local suburban streets to the farm. You can imagine what this was like with lively young pigs wanting to explore and get away from the herd. It was the same routine as unloading from a truck at the farm with family and farmhands kitted out with sticks and boards to try and keep them going where we wanted. The secret was to be calm and quiet and just nudge a couple of them into starting off the way you wanted them to go and the rest would catch on. Fortunately, in our area the residents usually kept their gates shut so we didn't often have to retrieve stragglers from peoples' gardens.

We kept over three hundred of these young pigs and that includes about a hundred being kept up the road at Hough End. In later years, the pigs were fed on Pig Meal, a prepared pig food made by BOCM who will feature later in this story. However, in the days just after the war, fancy Pig Meals were hardly in use on Britain's farms and, like many others, ours got fed on swill plus a percentage of Kellogg's grains.

We use the word swill today as a verb to denote drinking greedily or sluicing something out. To those of us feeding pigs, swill was pig food made from kitchen waste. Mum's kitchen might have produced enough waste to feed one or two pigs, but we had hundreds. However, there were restaurants about that could supply our needs. Our supplier of choice was UCP or United Cattle Products who had a chain of restaurants and shops across the North West. UCP specialised in selling Tripe, Cow Heels and Ox tails. At their peak they had an unbelievable one hundred and forty-six outlets and there were always queues for seats in the restaurants. Today, I can't imagine even Jamie Oliver being able to promote a single outlet dedicated to feeding his customers on Tripe, Cow Heels and Oxtails!

Dad or one of the farmhands would go round to the UCP shops with empty dustbins and swap them for ones filled with kitchen waste. During the war, we also got waste food from a canteen that had been set up in St Werburgh's Church Hall about quarter of a mile away to feed American troops. The troops weren't fussy about keeping their cutlery out of their food waste and quite a lot of knives, forks and spoons stamped as being property of the U.S. Government had to be retrieved before it could be used to feed the pigs. My sister Linda has still got a couple of these strange souvenirs. The pigs would eat the waste food as delivered but Dad thought it was safer to cook it! So how do you cook large quantities of waste food for pigs? Well, by boiling it and that's where the boiler in the Yard came in.

What we had was a collection of about eight large beer barrels which had been acquired from one of Manchester's many breweries. The top 12 - 15 inches was then sawn off these so that the container left was just over 3 feet high. These were arrayed on three sides of a square and into each one was fitted a steam pipe with a tap to turn the steam on. The steam was piped to this array of barrels from the large boiler that lived in a boiler house in the Main Yard. When kitchen waste from UCP was delivered, the boiler would be lit, a dustbin full of waste would go into each barrel and it would be topped up with water. Once steam was raised, it would be piped into the barrels which would then boil gloopily for a few hours. After the swill had cooled down, it was then bailed out with buckets into a wheeled container that could tip. This could then be pushed into each sty in turn and tipped up to pour the swill into the troughs that were in each sty. It sounds disgusting, it smelt disgusting and it was disgusting. But how those piggy-wigs loved it and fought for their place at the trough. We were all glad when we switched to Pig Meal.

The other thing to think about is that three hundred pigs are also going to produce quantities of pig muck. Very large quantities. The pigsties were cleaned out regularly and the pig muck and bedding was dumped onto the midden in the Stackyard. It could have grown to ridiculous proportions were it not for the allotment holders of South Manchester. They wanted muck from our midden by the ton to dig into their allotments. We got a steady stream of people, especially at weekends, knocking on the door and wanting to buy up to 3 tons of muck for which they would hand over £1 per ton and leave us with the address of their plot. It became a regular job for my younger brother Oliver and me to load up the trailer for the Ferguson tractor and we often got into smelly muck fights when a bit flew off the forkful you were swinging towards the trailer and accidentally hit your brother. Honour had to be retrieved by an aimed gob of muck and it all went downhill from there. When we were a bit older, Oliver and I used to drive the tractor and trailer round to the allotments in question and tip it. When I say a bit older, I mean just that, as we were definitely under driving age at about fourteen or fifteen when we went delivering. Nobody seemed to mind but it was a different world then.

Another aspect of living on a farm in the suburbs was that children wanted to come and see the animals, which usually meant the pigs as we kept them away from the more exotic animals unless they were being escorted. They would come and knock at the door and say, "Please Mister, can we come and look at the pigs." They were usually told "Yes, but don't open any doors." To be fair, most of them were happy to do this but there were always those that could hear the pigs in the sties but couldn't see them properly because they weren't tall enough to look over the doors. So, they undid the bolt and opened the door. When they did this, the pigs would think someone was coming in to feed them, so they'd make a dash for the door to get to front of the queue and then they'd be out and away. Good kids would run back to the house to tell us what had happened, but most would just scarper. The first we'd know about it was when a neighbour would dash across the road shouting "The pigs are out!" Or a passing motorist having to swerve to avoid speeding pigs would come in to complain. So, it was on with wellies, grab sticks and off in pursuit. The damn things could get everywhere in no time at all.

We'd have grand round ups all over Chorlton and fortunately the local police took a fairly relaxed view of happenings around the farm. I think they found that our activities broke the monotony. They'd certainly join in with gusto when we'd got a far roaming pig pack to gather up. On one memorable occasion, I was with one of local bobbies when we spotted a young porker diving down a passage way between buildings. The pig heard us pounding after him and dived down a side ginnel only to find it was a dead end. "I've got him now" said the bobby and advanced steadily towards him while I hung back slightly. I don't know what the bobby thought he was going to do. Pick it up? Arrest it? The pig had other ideas and bolted straight between his legs tipping the bobby onto his back. I was laughing so much that I didn't even try to catch the pig as it sped past me. With his dignity ruffled I was told not to tell any of his colleagues what had happened.

On another occasion we had a police van and a car helping us round a bunch of renegade sheep that had jumped to freedom. The police all thoroughly enjoyed that escapade which I'll tell in full a little later.

Giselle-17

Chapter Seven
Dens, Gangs and Weapons

Like all kids, we formed into gangs to play games and we also needed gang HQ's, so dens were required. Most games involved trying to capture the opposing gang's HQ. Secret dens were much more exciting if you could manage to make one. On a farm there were opportunities for this. One lot used the old hen house in the Playground and the other gang used a shed that had been built with the salvaged timber from Parkers in the woodyard and surprise, surprise it was almost waterproof. It was certainly proof against the lumps of timber that might and did rain down on it when hurled at it by the opposition. There were dens in the lofts, dens in the haystacks, dens in the shrubbery in the middle of the massive, long clump of rhododendrons and we even planned an underground den on the island in the middle of the duck pond. Dad found out about this latter plan and it was very firmly vetoed. We also started to dig one in the Playground, but Mum used this area with washing lines as her drying ground so that also got vetoed in case she accidentally fell in. As a further deterrent, we were also told that there was a dead donkey buried there.

I only found out recently that the massive rhododendron clump that housed a den was there by accident. Dad and Uncle Seymour were at an auction in the 1930s and Dad put his hand up to bid for what he thought was twenty small rhododendron bushes that no-one else was interested in, so they were very cheap. When he brought the car and trailer round to load them. He found out that there was a misprint in the catalogue, and he'd bought two hundred! Uncle Seymour took a load of them and he gave a lot away but at Park Brow, he planted two parallel rows of them about 40 feet long so that they'd grow up to form a hedge between the decorative garden and the fruit garden. By the time that we kids were old enough to start exploring the garden, the two rows of rhododendrons had grown together to form one long clump with a tunnel down the middle that formed our den.

The reason we thought that we could build a den on the island in the middle of the duck pond was that we'd acquired boats of a sort. When Dad wanted some replacement barrels for boiling swill in, he'd get hold of some very large barrels from a local brewery – probably Hydes, which was our nearest. To use them for boiling swill, they cut off the top 15 inches of each barrel. These off cuts would nowadays be used to make smart planters for the garden. What we found out was that we could roll them to the duck pond and float them. There was much very wet experimentation until we learnt how to balance in the things. This was when found out the pond was only about 2 feet deep. What Mum thought of the state of us when we came in with soaking wet socks and trousers has regrettably never been recorded. Once we'd learned how to balance in the barrel boats, we got makeshift paddles scrounged from the wood pile and set off paddling round the circular duck pond and out to the little round island in the middle. We had to have races of course and that naturally led to more falling in as we strained to get more speed from our vessels. Unsurprisingly the whole enterprise got banned on the grounds that we were disturbing the ducks and our boats got broken up.

Gangs of us and our friends from both school and the neighbourhood formed and re-formed into different groups depending on what game we were playing. Cap pistols and small bows and arrows were our weapons and long lengths of timber from the wood pile made spears or pikes. How no-one got seriously hurt was a miracle, especially when as we got older, we graduated to air guns and bigger bows. To be fair, the air guns that Dad bought us were pretty Mickey Mouse affairs that took ages to load and could possibly fire a slug for 15 yards with a following wind. We were strictly told to only fire them at targets, but in the heat of combat the rules got ignored. My old friend Paul Brown used to tell people for forty years after the event that I'd once shot him in the backside. When he dropped his trousers immediately after the incident, so the wound could be examined, all there was was a bright red spot that became a bit of a bruise later, which tells you how weak the airgun was. I told him that if he'd surrendered when I challenged him instead of trying to run for it, it wouldn't have happened, but he still complained. In later years we had access to proper air rifles, but we knew just how powerful these were and never pointed them anywhere near anyone.

One of our more stupid games was playing at being Knights of Old. This entailed us kitting ourselves out with dustbin lids as shields and Mum's clothes props as lances. Then mounting our bicycles and trying to steer our bikes hands free, we'd try to joust, starting in the cinder surfaced stubby bit of Cavendish Road opposite the farm. With minimal control of our bikes it was chaotic at best and I once lost control and found myself charging Don Quixote-like at the telephone box on the corner of Sandy Lane. It ended with the clothes prop breaking a window in the phone box and going through, leaving me dangling on the end of my lance for a moment before it broke. What happened next is best covered by the phrase "Tiptoe quietly away and admit nothing".

Fireworks acquired during the run up to Bonfire Night were used during our skirmishes. There were penny bangers, three-halfpenny bangers and the big, much prized Standard 'Cannons' that cost tuppence. There was a fun item called a Flying Imp which was like a miniature rocket but with no stick. These you were supposed to place on a flat surface, light the fuse and then run off for a safe distance. These would fizz into life then hurl themselves through the air in crazy gyrations for about ten seconds. Great fun but highly unpredictable as to where they'd end up. So, when sneaking up on 'The Enemy's' den, bangers would be lit then hurled like hand grenades to scare the other gang out and then Flying Imps would be hurled in their general direction to scatter them. Then we could dive in and capture their Den. Another win for our side.

We managed to create 'artillery' in this period. Oliver had a pair of tubular stilts and I had a pogo stick which also was based on a round tube. We experimented by dropping lighted 'bangers' down the tubes and enjoyed the resulting bang, flash and plume of smoke that came out the end. Next stage was to get some clay from down near the banks of the Brook and roll it into balls just big enough to fit snugly down the tubes. Let the clay balls dry overnight, then get your stilt, light a banger and drop it down inside followed by a clay ball and hold the stilt at an angle with the base on the ground. There was a satisfying bang and a shower of broken clay bits came flying out of the end – some flying for as much as 25 yards. With better projectiles we could do better and experimented with marbles – not very good as they weren't a tight enough fit in the barrel. Best were some wooden balls off an old skittle game which were quite a close fit and I saw a couple of them go flying for almost 100 yards down the field opposite.

The other thing that bangers were good for was making Depth Charges. We discovered quite by accident that the fuse on a lit banger doesn't go out when dropped into water. They floated on the surface still fizzing merrily then went off spraying water about. Now suppose we tried that in a bucket of water with a weight to sink the banger to the bottom...? A small flat stone and a rubber band did the trick and this time, there's a mighty thudding *Boom* and great column of water shot in the air. We didn't know it at the time, but we'd just discovered that water is incompressible. A few more booms in a bucket now using clay moulded into a ball on the end of the banger to make it sink and we were getting good at this. Then we split the seams on one bucket so on to bigger things. Let's Depth Charge the duck pond. A tuppenny Cannon in the duck pond made a very satisfying thud and you could feel the ground shake.

Excellent fun. We were in the Atlantic depth charging U-boats. Then the bucket with split seam was found and explanations were required. We said that we'd stopped doing it in a bucket and were bombing the duck pond instead. After one demonstration of our skills in Depth Charging, we were banned as Dad feared that we'd crack the concrete liner of the duck pond.

Being a farm, there were guns about for the control of vermin and when we were older, Oliver and I were gradually allowed to use them. There was a .410 shotgun (called a Four-Ten) which fired cartridges about half the size of a Twelve Bore. It was known as a Poacher's model and, with an extra press on the latch that opened the gun up for loading, it would fold completely in half so that it could be tucked out of sight into an inside jacket pocket.

"What? Me off poaching with a fire arm Officer? Can you see one?"

There was also a rather nifty device that got used when we were ratting. It looked rather like a blaggers sawn off shot gun or a double-barrelled highwayman's pistol. It had two short barrels about a foot long and a small shaped stock to fit in your hand. It took two Four-Ten cartridges so didn't have big kick and, being short barrelled, it was ideal to swing round quickly to take a shot at a fleeing rat. Its downside was it was not hammerless like modern shotguns and there was always the fear that you'd catch one of the hammers on your clothing and fire it accidentally.

The other gun that Oliver and I used was one that had been 'liberated' by one of our local tradesmen during his time in Germany at the end of WW2. It was called a garden gun and was unusual in that it had a .22 rifle for its left-hand barrel and 9mm shotgun barrel on the right. So, you could use the rifle at longer range targets and the shotgun up close, I remember it having a beautifully shaped stock, so it was very comfortable to use, and, unlike shotguns, it had sights which were set up for the rifle barrel. This too was a hammer gun, so you had to be careful with it as Oliver found out when he shot himself in the foot with it after he caught the hammer of the shotgun barrel on his coat. It made a nasty mess of his foot but as it was only a little 9mm shot cartridge, it didn't blow great chunks off his foot. A narrow escape.

The other bits of weaponry that we played with were provided by Bob. When doing his National Service, he became a corporal and a weapons instructor and subsequently turned up at home with "Toys" for Oliver and me to play with. These were such items as .303 rifle bullets in clips, a Hand Grenade and a Mortar Bomb. All of these were disarmed practice items but scored many 'Cool' points with friends. One day he even brought home a German Schmeisser machine pistol that some squaddie must have liberated during the war. Schmeissers are the sub machine guns that you always see nasty Germans toting in war movies. It had lost its magazine but could be made to fire single rounds so he demonstrated it by firing off odd rounds from one of the bedroom windows in the house into straw bales in the barn opposite. Fearsome. It was quickly returned to the armoury at Bob's base camp.

Chapter Eight
Playtime

In the aftermath of the war, all sorts of stuff was being sold off as Army surplus and Dad bought some odd bits which enlivened our lives. First off were a couple of good size kites, one of which was a hideous yellow colour with aluminium poles and was apparently used to lift meteorological instruments up to a reasonable altitude. This flew well but wasn't a patch on the 'Big Un' which was about 6 feet high with a 6 feet span. The front was like a triangular section box kite, but it also had large triangular wings as well. This kite was made of plain white fabric with poles made of some light but very tough wood. At the time, we didn't know what the armed forces used it for but guessed that it might have been used to haul signals aerials aloft as it had enormous lift. As small children, we weren't allowed to fly it alone or we would have been lifted off the ground. We could fly it when we were older and heavier but had to have a substantial handle on the reel of cord to hold onto or it would have ripped out of our hands.

Over 50 years after we first flew it, it was still surviving and went to a good home. A local country park was holding a Kite Festival managed by a Kite Club, so I went and asked someone if they'd be interested in owning the 'Big Un' as a bit of history. They were very chuffed when they saw it as they'd seen drawings of one but never the real thing. It was apparently used in the War to lift up the radio aerials of off shore power boats such as MTB's and Air/Sea Rescue launches. They told me that they gave talks on kites to schools and clubs and could use it as a visual aid when telling the story of kites. I hope it's still giving good service.

Another bit of Forces surplus kit that had a long life was the airman's rescue dinghy. You'll have seen the sort of thing in war movies with an unhappy, damp airman seated in it waiting for rescue. We used it on warm summer days at home as an inflatable paddling pool. The ubiquitous plastic things that every family has in their back garden now just didn't exist then, so our paddling pool was unique and popular with local kids. It also got taken on holiday with us for quite a few years and bobbed about in the waves of the Irish Sea with family and friends hanging off it.

The fourth and final army surplus item was a huge sledge. Well it seemed huge to us because we were only small, but you could certainly park half a dozen kids on it. Quite what the Army wanted with a large sledge, we couldn't imagine. Possibly it was built for some planned campaign in Norway. Anyway, it was certainly big with wide flat runners that turned up at each end and a semi-circular hoop at each end like fenders. The whole thing was fastened together with strips of leather or cord and there didn't seem to be any nails or screws used in its construction. It was very light considering its size and had the curious name of "Nansen Mod." stencilled onto it. Perhaps it was modelled on the sledges used by Nansen on his Arctic explorations and it looked like the sort of thing that you saw in old movies being dragged across the ice by some guy wrapped in furs. It was used intermittently by the family as we had no decent long snowy slopes near us, and it wasn't great at short slopes because the overhanging hoops at the front would dig in as you reached the bottom of a slope. A couple of times it was harnessed up to a pony and we went up and down the snowy roads in it though steering was only possible by putting a foot down. Its last outing was after I got married and I towed the sledge with my wife and a couple of friends aboard down a snowy lane behind a Land Rover. After that, it was stored in an outside shed and wood worm ate it away. A sad end to a fine bit of kit.

Another great Playtime memory is of the mighty swing. Dad had had enough of the typical swings that you could buy as they got battered to death in short order by the hordes of kids playing on them. Dad went out and acquired two telegraph poles which he cut down to about 15 feet in length and then set them in concrete about 5 feet apart in the playground. Helped by John Hallsworth, the blacksmith at Hough End, he fashioned some steel bar into large U – bolts with threads on the ends to take large nuts. Two of these were to be fixed into a hefty piece of oak that formed the top of the swing frame and two more were fixed into another large piece of oak that made the seat. Then he made ropes out of one-and-a-half-inch thick hemp that he spliced around galvanised eyes and the U-bolts were passed through the eyes and bolted down to the seat and the top beam. We had a swing. An uber swing. Ten kids could clamber on it with no chance of anything breaking. You couldn't tip that thing over by swinging too high. For that matter, Oliver and I couldn't swing it at all until we were about nine or ten because the seat was so heavy that we couldn't generate enough swing with our legs to get it going! What you did do was keep well clear when it was swinging as if that seat hit you, you really knew about it. It saw all us children into adulthood and was used by Linda, Susan and Bob's children when they were visiting the farm years later.

All the above may seem pretty simple stuff to children of today but all those years ago, there were no computer games and consoles and very few toys were made out of plastic. They were mostly made of metal, wood or cardboard and for boys, you could choose between cars, boats, trains, planes or board games. There wasn't much else. Dinky toys were popular and Hornby model trains. Boats were mostly powered by clockwork and planes you built yourself from balsa wood and tissue paper. Bob was always good with his hands and built some great planes. If you had an engine, as he did, you could build control line planes that flew round you in a circle while you controlled the elevators to make it do stunts. You could also build 'Free flight' models which you could launch and hope that you got them back. Bob had a big ugly one called Frankenstein that had his name, address and phone number written on it in case it flew out of sight. Radio control gear was possible but very expensive and very heavy so at that time, only really suitable for pretty big models. Bob also built some big model gliders which we helped him to fly. With their 6-foot wingspan, these really could fly literally for miles if let. However, his best one was fitted with a device that made it turn in a circle once it was released from the line that had towed it aloft and I've seen it stay up there circling, for quarter of an hour on a warm day gradually drifting further and further away as the wind shifted it. A splendid sight.

Another great product of the 1950s/60s was Jetex. This was nothing less than rocket power for boys! Can you imagine turning children loose today to play with real live rocket motors? You had a little aluminium tube that contained a slow burning propellant that was ignited by a fuse. The propellant gave off volumes of gas for 15 to 20 seconds that was ejected with some force from a nozzle. The motor units were very light and only about 4 centimetres long and you could very easily mount them in boats, cars and planes. I had some ridiculously fast model boats, but they were best in model planes as they could accelerate your plane up to some speed and height from which it would glide down so you got a good long flight for your money. The original Jetex motors and kits could be bought in toyshops and although these originals have long since disappeared, modern equivalents have appeared for dedicated aero modellers.

Down on the ground, injection moulding of plastics had arrived and with it the first Airfix models and plastic moulded cars instead of castings or tinplate. Up to then, if you wanted a model car, you got a die-cast Dinky or a tinplate one made in the US Zone of Germany. Tri-ang launched a very successful competitor to Hornby trains in the shape very accurately bodied model trains made in plastic. Oliver and I had quite a large Tri-ang train set that got passed on to Bob's son Paul and we also had a whole air force of plastic model planes hung from our bedroom ceiling. We had the odd clockwork boat that we motored round the duck pond and Bob had a beautifully made large electric powered motor launch that had been made by the famous firm of Bassett-Lowke. The electric motor was slow revving and heavy and the 6-volt lantern battery that it needed to drive it was heavy too, so despite its rakish appearance, its progress was stately and not sprightly. A few years later, long after Bob had finished playing with it and lost interest, I re-engined it with a model aircraft compression-ignition engine just to see how fast it would go. With the engined throttled back, it sped rapidly round the duck pond so, seeking more speed, I opened the throttle. A bad plan. The torque of the engine and propeller was such that the instant that I let go of it, it whipped over and sank as it rotated itself round the propeller. I recovered it but didn't tell Bob until years later when he asked what had happened to it.

Chapter Nine

Away at The Seaside – And on To School

Like many families at the time, we had an annual holiday for a fortnight at the seaside and in our case, it was initially at St Annes-on-Sea near Blackpool. Dad could only spare the time off from the farm to stay for a week, but he drove the rest of the family there for a week before he joined us. We stayed in the Park View Hotel which was well named as it actually overlooked the big park in the middle of St Annes. We went there from the late 1940s to about 1952.

St Annes had good beaches, a nice promenade with a boating pool on it and the much larger Fairhaven Lake at the end of the prom. At Fairhaven, you could hire motor boats to drive around one part of the lake if you were old enough. If you weren't, you had to hire a Duck. These were strange devices that looked like an oversize plastic duck for the bath but were equipped with a set of bicycle pedals that drove a propeller and a steering wheel. The was a cafe on the site that sold very good ice cream. Linda, Susan and Robert helped Mum to look after Oliver and me and there were donkey rides, trips into Blackpool and each year, an evening visit to the Variety Show held in the Park Pavilion. Very exotic to an eight or nine-year-old.

Oliver driving a Duck Boat with our cousin Vivienne in the next boat
That's me peering underneath the Duck's beak

Each year while at St Annes, Dad would buy Oliver and me a treat from the toy shop in town. Worden's was a toy treasure trove, always stocking really terrific toys that you didn't see elsewhere. It was great just to go inside and look at the stock while thinking about the something special that we could choose. Model boats were often chosen by me because there was the boating pool on the prom to sail them in. One that I can remember was a really good model called the Glenbur Submarine. Strangely, this was rubber powered and had to be wound up in a special stand before use but would run for a very long time. It could be made to run on the surface, run submerged or porpoise in and out of the water which was always preferred. I also had a fine tin-plate liner and a model of Malcolm Campbell's Bluebird boat that were bought in other years, but they didn't compare with the thrill of watching that submarine diving and surfacing as it sped across the pond on its way to overwhelm a hapless toy yacht! Das Boot!

Oliver was very thoughtful in his selection of a 'special' toy from Wordens and chose some superb model lorries. They were made by a firm called Shackleton between 1948 and 1952 and were beautifully engineered models of Foden lorries with pressed steel chassis frames and die cast cabs and backs. They could be completely disassembled with the spanners provided as they were all bolted together. Over three years he acquired a six-wheeler lorry, a tipper truck and a four-wheel trailer. They were built to last and he's still got them over sixty years later. I see similar ones appear occasionally on *Flog It* or other antiques shows, and they always sell for several hundred pounds. A smart investment for a seven-year-old.

After St Annes, Dad and Mum decided to go to the Isle of Man instead and so we flew into Ronaldsway airport and were taken by taxi to Port St Mary in the south of the island to stay at the Balqueen Hydro Hotel. Port St Mary was a quiet little fishing village with its own small fishing fleet that caught herrings that were then turned into the famous Manx Kippers in the smokehouse down by the harbour. The beach area was lovely and quite separate from the fishing harbour although both were part of the same bay. The beach was backed up to a sea wall and that had a promenade running along the top of it. Above the prom was quite a steep bank that was planted with fuchsia and hibiscus and had zig-zag paths through it leading up to the road above where all the hotels sat.

The Balqueen was a big hotel and must have catered for about two hundred guests. It was by far the biggest hotel in Port St Mary and its great cream painted frontage dominated the top road and the whole beach area. It was a completely different experience to St Annes as the Balqueen offered a complete family holiday package with all meals included, entertainments each evening and assorted activities each day. Your stay at the Balqueen was all about being entertained and they had an Entertainments Manager to organise activities for all ages to fill your day. Their Entertainments Manager was a really great guy named Fred Hoyle whose face looked like the result of a collision between a bulldog and a brick wall. He must have been in his 60s but had boundless energy and really threw himself into keeping the guests amused and he always had time for children of all ages. During the day, there were walks, cycle rides, treasure hunts plus tennis, bowls and golf matches. In the evenings there were dances, concerts, fancy dress competitions and coach trips to the theatre or cinema in Douglas. Fred's enthusiasm was so infectious that he had no trouble in getting everyone to take part.

Dining at the Balqueen with Fred Hoyle
(L to R) Mum, Susan, Dad, Oliver, Bob, Me, Linda, Fred

Fred led the weekly cycle ride to Rushen Abbey which was about 8 miles away. Fred had his own bike but everyone else hired one from a little cycle hire shop about 100 yards from the hotel for 2/6p (12 ½ p). The bikes were roadworthy but elderly and you were very lucky if you managed to find one with a Sturmey Archer 3 speed gear. About forty to fifty of us would set off behind Fred (and you went in front of him at your peril!) and those who didn't want to cycle could take a coach to the Abbey. When you got there, the Abbey gardens were laid out with verandas and a dance floor, so people could dance to the resident trio and tuck into a strawberry cream tea for which the place was famous. There was a play area for younger ones that included a most unusual roundabout. It was water powered! Once everyone was aboard the little carriages, someone would open a sluice and start a water wheel going that drove it round. Very nifty.

For the return cycle journey, the route took us through a ford near the Abbey with a foot bridge alongside. The local kids knew that our hotel sent a group on bikes on Wednesdays, so they'd sometimes put bricks in the roadway under water. If you hit a brick, you were off and got a soaking. The wild ones among us youngsters would take a flying run at the ford and lift our legs in the air to fly through in a cloud of spray. The sane way was to pedal steadily through, hoping that you'd miss any stones and that it hadn't rained recently so the level of the river was low. This way you could get through dry shod. Needless to say, the fun option was to be one of those to get across the ford first. Then you could stand on the footbridge cheering or groaning at the efforts of others.

The Sunday morning walk to the Sound of Man (the narrow strip of water between the main Island and the Calf of Man) – led by Fred of course - was always well attended and we always got rewarded for taking part with ice creams and bottles of pop at the cafe there. As at Rushen Abbey, many of the residents would go to the Sound of Man by coach to join the others and if you didn't fancy the walk back or it was raining, you could hop on a coach. Funny. It just never seemed to rain! One of the other weekly events that we enjoyed was the Fancy Dress Competition as there were decent prizes to be won. Oliver and I were always entered by Mum who was very competitive, and Bob sometimes took part. Mum performed miracles with crepe paper, cardboard and Sellotape and I seem to have innumerable photos of us taking part. Our children roar with laughter at these photos and think we look like complete prats. Looking at the old photos from these holidays, it's clear that family friends and neighbours sometimes came with us and we got to know well some families who came regularly in the same fortnight as us.

Dad loved his fishing and always took his sea angling equipment with him. He used to hire a local boatman to take him and a few friends round the south coast towards the Calf of Man and come back with Pollock that he'd caught These he'd get cooked in the kitchen at the hotel. I went with him once and was very seasick on the way out as the 'Teddy' was only a small boat and the sea near the Calf could get very choppy. Then we stopped and started to fish. It was a bit calmer and John Gawne, the boatman, lent me a Mackerel rod with a load of feathers attached to the hooks. I hung this over the side and lifted it up and down as instructed and to my astonishment caught several Mackerel. A fishing first. On the way back to Port St Mary, John the boatman let me take the helm of the boat while he, Dad and his friends swapped tall fishing tales. I saw something in the water that looked a bit like a shark's triangular fin but there was another smaller one close behind. A shark and a youngster? I turned the boat slightly off course, aiming to head between them and was getting pretty close when John looked up and saw where we were heading. He stepped smartly forward and turned the helm so that we missed them and then he told me "You just missed running over a Basking Shark!" Wow! As we passed close by, I saw how big it was and realised that it would not have been a one-sided collision if I had hit it.

Not fancying another puke making boat trip, I settled for fishing with a simple square frame to wind the line round with a weight and a hook and this I first used from the breakwaters round the fishing port without much success. However, just round the corner from the port were some fine ledges that jutted out into the sea that were great for fishing from. I was there once, and the water was crystal clear, so I could see a huge Conger Eel slithering about on the sea bottom among the seaweed. I baited the hook with a piece of limpet that I'd bashed off a rock and also tied a lure to the line just above the hook. The lure was half a set of false teeth that I'd picked out of a rock pool and when fastened to the line and pulled slowly through the water, it jiggled about in what I hoped was an enticing manner. I hurled the weighted line as far out as would go then slowly pulled in the line trying to drag it close to the Conger. It worked. The Conger dived for the false teeth, I gave a sharp tug on the line to get him hooked and then battle commenced. He was a big old boy and was well over 3 feet long, so it took a lot of effort to work him round to a place where the ledges were shallow, and I could drag him ashore. We carried it back to the hotel to show the family the mighty monster that I'd caught, and everyone was most impressed. Especially about the false teeth.

I used to wonder where the false teeth had come from. Were they the last remnants of some poor drowned sailor man? Had a fellow fisherman slipped on the rocks and had his false teeth knocked loose in the fall? I decided that they'd most probably been lost at sea when someone had been horribly seasick on the Isle of Man Ferry and lost both his lunch and his teeth.

Looking back on holidays like this at a distance of 60 years, we all really enjoyed ourselves even as 'just becoming teenagers' and were excited to know that we'd be going back next year and meeting again the friends that we'd made. It was simple fun but I'm not sure how it would go down with ten to fourteen-year-olds today.

There was a spin-off from our holidays in the Isle of Man and that was in Dad and Mum's choice of a school for Oliver and me to go to after we'd finished at our primary. They'd not been at all impressed with the school near Preston that Bob had been to as a boarder, so they were looking for somewhere else. They found it in the shape of King Williams College on the Isle of Man right next door to Ronaldsway Airport that we flew into from Manchester. You couldn't miss it from the windows of the plane as you approached for landing with its tall clock tower and grey granite walls. It looked not unlike Parkhurst Prison on the Isle of Wight! Anyway, that's where Oliver and I finished up our schooldays.

King Williams College seen from the seashore

Both Oliver and I had initially gone to a private school in Didsbury called Moor Allerton School about two and half miles away from the farm. It was called a Preparatory School rather than a primary school as its aim was to prepare its pupils for the Common Entrance Exam to get them into Public Schools. It was a very good school with good teachers and a friendly atmosphere and it's still going strong today. I made very good friends there who remained friends until adulthood and we all got together during school holidays. Chris, who I still see almost seventy years later; Dave who later memorably slid his Fiat down Mottram hill on its roof; Frank, Mark and of course Nelson. Nelson was rather disapproved of by Dad because his father, also called Nelson, was a Theatrical Agent and therefore, in Dad's eyes at least, likely to mix with a raffish theatrical crowd. In practice, this hardly happened though Nelson senior did get take a few of us to Blackpool Tower Circus and then got us backstage and we were introduced to the famous circus clown Charlie Cairoli. A few years later, Nelson's dad also booked the gorgeous Tiller girls into a show in Manchester so meeting them was a thrill at the age of eighteen or so. Rather more exciting was driving across Manchester in the old Standard Vanguard pick-up truck with two attractive Tiller girls squeezed between Chris and me on the front bench seat. I was steering and working the pedals while one of the Tillers was changing gear with the column gear change. We were packed in so tightly that if I'd tried to use the column gear lever myself, I'd surely have got my face slapped.

After Moor Allerton, I went to King Williams College in 1955 and Oliver joined me in 1957. We travelled there by plane from Manchester Airport flying in elderly Douglas DC 3s (also known as Dakotas). King Williams College (KWC) is best known for its fiendish General Knowledge Paper which is still published every Christmas in the Guardian with answers published at the end of January. This quiz has now been going for over one hundred years and questions today are cunningly phrased to fox Googlers. What outsiders probably don't realise was that we pupils had to do the damn thing. Twice! We had to do it unseen like an exam for a timed period before the break for Christmas, then take the paper home, try to find the answers, then have to do it all over again under exam conditions after the holidays having hopefully memorised the answers. It was not a popular item in the schools year, except among the swots and smartasses!

Me and Oliver descending from a Douglas Dakota (DC3) for another term

KWC was, and still is, a good competent school sending a lot of its scholars onto university but the make up of the school population has changed considerably. In my time, most pupils came from middle class families in the North West with a smattering of boys from families who were living around the world but who wanted a UK education for their children. An example of this was the Higgins brothers from Venezuela though they actually originated from Bogota in Colombia. The younger brother was Henry Higgins and, far from starring in My Fair Lady, gained fame by becoming a professional bull fighter whom the Spanish nick-named El Ingles. Poor Pancho as we knew him, survived the bullring only to die in a hanggliding accident at the age of thirty-four. The school today has a greatly reduced number of boarders with many of the students coming from overseas and is co-educational. We were kept well away from girls!

The boarding away from home bit was a bit tough to put up with at first but you soon learned that school would determine just about everything that happened in your life from then on. The trick was to think of ways of evading the system so that you could do your own thing. Examples of this that I pulled off were avoiding the Combined Cadet Force (CCF) with its blanco and 'bull' by joining the Scouts, avoiding playing cricket by playing golf and getting out of a lot of rugby by volunteering to do gardening for one of the housemasters. To most of us raised on a diet of WW2 films about Prisoners of War, we were doing the same thing as the PoW's and trying to beat the system. The chances of escape though, were very much slimmer than at Colditz because even if you ran away from school, you couldn't get off the island. During the war, the Internees and PoW's on the Isle of Man found out the same thing! I persuaded my parents to pay to have my bike shipped over to school and this gave me a lot more mobility in the short free periods that we were allowed. For mobility read opportunity to get well away from school for a crafty smoke or occasionally to meet up with girls. We kept out of pubs however because they would always report us.

With friends I did assorted daft things and one of our better stunts was interrupting the rehearsal for a play that was being produced by our house master, one George Charles Kelly who was always known as 'Drac'. The rehearsal was taking place on the stage at the end of the school hall. Above the hall, but unknown to most was a loft than ran all the way along the hall but then stopped right above the stage so anyone in the loft could lean over the edge and see onto the stage. A couple of us had found the entrance to the loft and explored the clutter of stuff stored up there and also found out that it gave access onto the roof. On a fine night, it was a good safe place to nip out to for an uninterrupted smoke with no smell of ciggy smoke to give you away. Among the junk in the loft we unearthed two or three chamber pots, so we decided to lower one down towards the stage on a piece of string and set it swinging during one of Kelly's rehearsals. Timing was important if we were to get away with it, but we knew that Kelly was in the habit of pacing up and down the length of the hall just listening to the performances. One of us was in the loft with chamber pot ready and the other was watching through a gap in the door to the hall waiting for Kelly to start one of his walks away from the stage. The signal was given, the chamber pot lowered and started in a swing just above the performers heads. Then it was time to scarper swiftly down from the loft and away into the nearby library where we could pretend to be reading. We'd just got into the library when we heard Kelly's bellow of rage. The players on the stage had seen nothing as the pot was swinging a few feet above their heads and no-one had noticed until Kelly turned round and saw it. He was shouting imprecations and searching round for the perpetrators who he imagined were the back-stage crew. Everyone was convulsed with laughter except Kelly. He couldn't find out who'd done it and never did.

When boys were leaving for the last time to go on to university or wherever, they'd often carry out practical jokes on their last evening in school before disappearing for good the following morning. Two stick out in my mind, the second one of which was bit cruel considering who it was played on. The other was played on Kelly, who richly deserved it. Kelly was enormously proud of his TV set because he'd got superb reception as a result of paying to have a TV aerial mounted on the top of the school tower with a lead going all the way down to his study. One boy among the many who disliked Kelly and his unpleasant ways, decided to get his revenge which was both simple and diabolical. He got into the school tower and, a short way up, he stuck a pin right through Kelly's aerial cable thus shorting the aerial out. He apparently snipped off the ends of the pin, so it couldn't be seen. Kelly's TV reception was ruined, and they never found the pin, so all the aerial cable had to be replaced. I only found out about that story after I'd left school and gone to a reunion in Manchester a couple of years later.

The other trick was the cruel one because it was played on Taffy Pritchard, the wood working teacher, who was a really nice guy. It was just unlucky for him that he owned the smallest car among the staff in the shape of a little Renault 4CV. We had Fives Courts at school which are a bit like Squash Courts except that the back wall is not a complete wall. The roof of a

69

Fives Court slopes down from the high front wall until it's about 8 feet off the ground at the back of the court. The back wall is only about 3 feet high with a door in the middle to let players into the court so that there's a gap about 5 feet high between the top of this small back wall and the lower edge of the roof. A large gang of rugby players pushed Taffy's little Renault up to the back wall of one if the Fives Courts and then man handled it over the wall and into the court. Perfectly practical for a dozen strong youths but next day, everyone had gone home so there's no-one there to get it out. Poor Taffy was left with his car stranded in a space that you couldn't even get a crane into to lift it out. They had to demolish part of the back wall to release it.

Oliver and I used to fly to and from school at the start and end of each term, but we weren't allowed off the Island at half term. Whenever possible, Mum would fly across at half term and stay with us at a hotel which was a nice break and a couple of times when she couldn't make it, I was put up by friends who lived on the Island and once by some rather distant relatives who also lived there.

The old Dakotas were run by BEA (British European Airways) who were the government sponsored airline at the time for flights within Europe so they were well turned out and reliable but they only flew at about 10,000 feet so you often got tossed about by turbulence and air pockets. The worst flight I ever had to or from Ronaldsway airport was a scary one from Edinburgh back to the Island in a Bristol Freighter run by Silver City. This flight went through a thunderstorm and, although everyone was strapped in, the plane was being thrown about in all directions and so hand baggage flew out of the racks and was flying through the air and hitting passengers for about fifteen minutes as it tumbled up and down the aisle. We were so busy hanging on we didn't have to time to be frightened. I then knew why the RAF nicknamed the plane *'The Bristol Frightener'*.

A latter day spin off from being at a public school is that today, my friends rib me about what went on there. Particularly since they learned that we had a Matron for each dormitory who looked after the mundane tasks of getting our clothes washed and ironed, sewing on buttons or darning socks. This was a cue for loads of *'Carry On...'* comments of the "Ooohh Matron" sort or "What else did she do for you?" Nudge, nudge. Well the answer is boringly enough – nothing. The Matrons were chosen for being motherly types rather that for their beauty, so we were just glad to have them around doing the housekeeping as it were.

The other subject that intrigues my friends is fagging. Did I do fagging? Did I have a fag? Answer to both is yes. Fagging was one of the ways that we kept our allocated areas of the school tidy. All boys were allocated tasks such as sweeping out the common rooms or going litter picking around the grounds. You got relief from jobs like this as these tasks were also used as punishment for those who broke the rules. You could get told to do a week, a fortnight or a month of litter picking or sweeping for some infringement and the boy whose allocated task it was got time off. Prefects (who we called Praepositors) were allocated personal fags who would clean their shoes or tidy out their study. They also cooked at weekends doing simple stuff like beans on toast as a suppertime time treat, which the fag was usually allowed to share. Prefects were the ones who policed the day to day running of the school in line with the rules laid down by the teaching staff. Prefects thus led privileged lives as fellow prefects wouldn't shop you for doing stuff that you shouldn't, such as smoking, drinking or seeing girls unless you were stupidly blatant about it.

During this period from 1955 to1960, Oliver and I were only helping out on the farm during the holidays, but we were still expected to do our bit. However, I had time to collect my tractor driving licence and later my full driving licence during the longer summer holidays. And then it was time for university and a complete change of life.

Chapter Ten
Strange Animals

Dad always loved animals and couldn't resist keeping strange ones if they were offered. Apart from those circus elephants during the war. He was almost entirely self-taught in Zoology and Botany yet became a Fellow of the Royal Zoological Society and could identify most plants, trees and animals that he came across in life or in pictures. He loved teasing his mother in law and one day he brought home a sack that wiggled and on being asked what it was, he told her it was a snake. This quite naturally invoked a "Don't be ridiculous Leonard" from Grandma. Whereat he cut the tie and tipped a small python on the floor. Never again did she ask him what he had brought home.

He regularly took us to Belle Vue Zoo in Manchester where he was well known and was often allowed to parts of the zoo that the general public weren't allowed in. Though we didn't know it at the time, Linda's husband-to-be Peter was working at the Zoo as an assistant keeper during his university vacations. A few years later after they were married, this association with a zoo paid off when they were holidaying in Ireland. Linda and Peter went to Dublin Zoo and, after Peter had explained his zoo-keeping credentials, they were allowed 'backstage' and asked if they would like to see the Lion cubs. Dublin Zoo at that time had one of the best lion breeding programmes in the world and Linda was offered a chance to hold a couple of cubs.

Linda with Lion Cubs at Dublin Zoo

With regular visits by Oliver and me to Belle Vue Zoo, at a very early age we could distinguish between a dromedary and a Bactrian camel, but recognising Wildebeest from Hartebeest was beyond me. Dad had a large library which he devoured and was always buying more books about animals and plants. I have an early recollection of standing watching him making more book shelves which were quickly filled. I once had to do a project at school about trees and their leaves and he took me on an expedition around local parks, woods and the garden while we collected as many different leaves as we could find. He showed me how to identify them from his books so that I could stick each leaf to a separate page and then write both its English and Latin names. I must have been only been about nine or ten, but I was very proud of the finished result and it taught me a lot about how to research facts in later life.

There was a local Poultry Keepers Association that Dad was a member of. This was a group that had originally kept the more unusual breeds of poultry such as bantams and exhibited them at local shows. During the war years, they were more about keeping breeding and laying stock and swapping chickens to keep their families supplied with eggs. After the war, they reverted to keeping fancy poultry and Dad acquired some interesting looking chickens from the members. He gave Oliver and me some Polish hens which were pretty little birds with speckled black and white feathers and very distinctive pom-poms of feathers covering their heads. There were other breeds as well such as Cochins that had feathers all the way down their legs so that they looked as if they were wearing trousers. It's likely that his association with the poultry keepers was what led him to join the Didsbury and South Manchester Agricultural Society of which more lately.

A scruffy looking Oliver with our Polish hens

I think it was the pictures in his books of ornamental pheasants that decided him to start keeping some as they were much more exotic than the fancy chickens. The pheasants turned out to be only the tip of the menagerie iceberg. Once he'd decided on keeping pheasants, he needed to find someone to buy them from and he located a chap called Robert Jackson who ran a business in nearby Timperley importing exotic animals and particularly birds. After a chat with Robert Jackson to check on what he needed to provide to keep pheasants, he came home to set about building suitable enclosures. He decided to put them at the side of the playground though this area was already occupied by a row of hutches for rabbits (and the odd ferret) which had been providing us with extra meat during the war. The hutches were moved down to Hough End farm and put in the care of Jimmy Ryan as mentioned earlier.

Dad built four enclosures initially, each with outdoor areas about 12 feet square and 7 feet high all covered in wire netting. Then there were sheltered areas at the back of each enclosure about 4 feet deep and the same 12 feet wide as the outdoor areas. The sheltered areas were planked on all sides and on the roof just leaving a gap about 3 feet wide in the centre of the front wall so that birds and minders could get in and out. They had perches fitted and deep shelves to provide a lowered covered area to encourage the birds to nest underneath.

He initially bought pairs of cock and hen pheasants of 4 varieties, Reeves, Golden, Silver and Lady Amherst who were soon strutting about happily in their new quarters. Dad meanwhile had become very good friends with Robert Jackson who incidentally later moved to North Wales and founded the Welsh Mountain Zoo. Robert was always trying him to get try some new birds or animals and over the years Dad acquired a pair of beautiful, stately Crowned Cranes, a splendid Toucan, a chatty Mynah Bird and cute Little Owls as well as other breeds of pheasants. On the animal front, we acquired Porcupines, Pere David's Deer, Soay Sheep and even Wallabies. We weren't sure whether Dad actually owned all these or was just looking after them because Robert Jackson hadn't got room at Timperley.

The porcupines were kept in one of the undercover pig cotes on the far side of the Yard and ate lots of vegetables and were fond of potatoes. They shed their quills fairly often and we used to gather them up as they were valuable trading commodities at school. They were pretty docile and didn't bother us when we went in to top up their food and water or change their bedding. They did have incredibly sharp teeth and one night gnawed a huge hole through the 1-inch thick planking on their door and escaped. They were rounded up next morning using long handles sweeping brushes to keep them from stabbing us.

The Pere David's deer didn't last long. They were only tiny little things, not much bigger than a spaniel but boy, could they jump! We turned them loose into the Tower Field which was pretty well fenced in to height of about 5 feet. They took one look at the fences, then took a short run and they were over and away and at least one of them was killed by a train when it jumped onto the tracks running beside the field. The surviving deer were corralled at the farm then returned to Robert Jackson.

The wallabies were interesting and entertaining but also prone to leap to freedom and so were also returned after a short fun filled stay. The Soay sheep were a rare breed and originated on the island of St Kilda way out on the Atlantic so were close in style to the wild sheep and goats found around the world with very large horns. They were also great escapists and got out of the Tower Field en masse. We set off after them and meanwhile someone had phoned the police, so they joined in. It was like the Wild West for about an hour and I have great memories of being driven at speed round Chorlton in the back of a police van with one bobby leaning out of the door trying to lasso a sheep that his driver was chasing up the road. No - he didn't succeed, but it was fun.

It was always a treat to go to Jackson's premises and see the incredible range of animals that he kept there ranging from beautiful brightly coloured finches to llamas – which can spit much farther that you'd think, as I once found out to my cost. A favourite was a lovely Sulphur Crested Cockatoo which greeted everyone who came near with a raucous "Hello Cocky". We would have loved to have it, but this was vetoed by Mother once she'd heard it. We already had a parrot anyway, an African Grey called Polly that lived in the corner of the kitchen and could mimic Dad's voice perfectly.

Polly was often let out his/her cage and would perch on the drying rack that hung from the kitchen ceiling with Mum complaining loudly and the rest of us keeping clear in case it decided to poop from on high. Sometimes it would perch on Dad's shoulder and nibble gently at his ear while Dad pretended that Polly was whispering to him secrets about what we children had been up to. Polly was usually fairly good tempered but one time, Uncle Eric Lou bent down to look at something near the cage and Polly got in a good bite at his ear. His language was spectacular.

This, by the way, was not my real Uncle Eric but a very old family friend who was always known as 'Uncle Eric' and he and his wife 'Aunty' Norah were godparents to Oliver and so very close to the family. They were really lovely people and we were all very fond of them. His real name was Eric Lewis, so he was known to us as Uncle Eric Lou to avoid confusion with the 'real' Uncle Eric. Uncle Eric Lou worked for an insurance company as an underwriter and sometimes investigator so had a fine fund of stories about assorted attempts to defraud the insurers. These were always told with much style and imagination and were always terminated by Uncle Eric's trademark "Eh?" followed by a mighty sniff as he twitched his nose.

Very pleased with his first four pheasant enclosures, Dad decided to build four more but, in addition to pheasants, he decided to keep more exotic fare. So, the toucan ended up in one in one and some little owls in another. I particularly remember the little owls because it was the job of Oliver and I to keep them fed. They liked live food so at first, we turned live mice out in their pen but, in an enclosed space, the owls weren't always successful in catching them. We found by experiment that they would eat freshly killed small animals, so we were asked to shoot a couple of sparrows a day with the air rifle. The owls tucked in to these quite happily.

Other memorable exotic birds that Dad acquired were peacocks. He had them at first at Park Brow, but we got fed up of being woken up by them with their very loud and raucous "*Miaow Miaow*" calls first thing in the morning. Far worse than roosters. They were exiled to Hough End where they strutted about for several years without being strangled by irate people living nearby. Uncle Will thought they were attractive things to have around and got a few for his farm in Wales but I don't know how long they survived there. The one good thing about them were the exotic tail feathers that they shed and these, along with porcupine quills, were high value trading commodities among school friends.

I mentioned the duck pond earlier and Dad's love of animals extended to waterfowl also. We had the usual farmyard staples of Muscovy ducks for their eggs and Aylesbury's for eating and they had the run of the farm at first. When the duck pond was built, the area around it was fenced off and the ducks were moved in. Then Dad started to acquire a few exotics. There were Bar Headed geese, Egyptian geese and Canada geese. For smaller ducks, Dad acquired beautifully coloured Carolina's and Mandarin's. This was pretty exotic fare for the suburbs of Manchester and there were always people wanting to see them. We also had a few Highland Cattle in the field across the road and these gave an unexpected Scottish look to South Manchester. Although plenty of people wanted to lean on the gate and look at them, nobody went in the field for fear of getting skewered on their massive horns. They were actually pretty gentle animals and they had a really cute and cuddly calf which got christened Teddy because he looked like an oversized teddy bear.

There was one other memorable bird that we acquired from Robert Jackson, but it wasn't one that Dad had particularly wanted. Robert Jackson had acquired an American Turkey Vulture and he was sure that Dad would like it. Dad didn't fancy it all. Whenever Dad went round to Jackson's, Robert would say, "Now how about this vulture, Len? I can do you a very good price." And Dad would always say "No". This went on for months and we assumed that Robert was trying to unload the beast at assorted zoos and was failing. One Sunday morning, I was with Dad in our old Standard Vanguard pick-up truck which as usual, had all sorts of stuff in the back covered by a tied down tarpaulin. We called in at one or two of our farming customers and then on the way home, called at Jackson's. I wandered round enjoying all the exotic animals and Dad went off for a cup of tea and a chat with Robert. After half an hour or so, Dad called to me and we got in the pickup and set off home.

After about 10 minutes Dad said, "I think the load may have shifted, I thought I heard something move in the back."

So, we stopped in a layby and pulled back to tarpaulin to reveal an extra item. A cage containing a bilious looking vulture. Dad grinned and said, "It looks like we've got ourselves a free vulture!"

We got the brute home and set it free in a spare pheasant enclosure where it hopped and flapped around for about five minutes before settling on its perch. Dad threw in some meat scraps and bones that were intended for the dogs and the vulture settled down and tucked in to these. With a butcher less than a quarter mile away, it looked like there would be no trouble keeping it fed.

"What shall we call it" asked someone. Dad went and looked up Turkey Vultures in one of his books and came back to announce that its Latin name was Cathartes Aura. We children thought that he'd said Cathartes Ora and immediately thought of Kia Ora, a well-known brand of orange squash. "That's it." said someone, "we'll call it Squashy!" And Squashy it stayed.

There was an excellent incident when Squashy met my Uncle Eric. This was my real Uncle Eric, father's younger brother and not Uncle Eric Lou. Uncle Eric was the shortest of the five brothers and was what I'd describe as a little bantycock sort of a chap who strutted around in old fashioned riding jodhpurs and reckoned that there wasn't much that you tell him. Like all my uncles, he was a great kidder and the five of the brothers would tell each other tall tales with straight faces, often with the deliberate intent of starting an argument. Seeing and hearing Dad and my uncles get into one of their arguments was a fine spectator sport – but you never interfered or offered an opinion or the five of them would turn on the outsider.

So, when Uncle Eric had a wander round the playground looking at the pheasants, he naturally said "What's in than one Len?" as he came to an apparently empty pen.

"A vulture" said Dad grinning slyly as he knew he wouldn't be believed.

"Don't be daft. You've never got a vulture!"

"Yes, I have!"

"Well where is it then?"

"It's inside. Probably sleeping on its perch."

"I don't believe you."

"Well go in and have a look for yourself."

"Right. I will."

Now this was one of the second lot of pheasant enclosures that Dad had built but in order to make them cosier for the birds, the opening into the sleeping enclosures was narrower and entry height was lower. So, you couldn't usually see the birds if they were inside unless you were right in front of the opening and ducked your head to look inside.

So, Uncle Eric opens the access door and goes into the outside area then walks across to the sleeping enclosure and sticks his head inside. Squashy is inside on his perch, and seeing an intruder, he gives a squawk and opens his wings. Uncle Eric gives a yell and jumps back forgetting that he's half inside a low height opening. He whacks his head, and staggers back uttering loud oaths. His head starts to bleed.

Dad, grinning hugely, says "you're bleeding Eric. You'd better get out quick. You know what vultures are like for blood!"

So, Uncle Eric hastens out, still dripping blood and raining curses. Mum patched him up and fed him tea while Squashy went back to sleep. We children were just collapsed with laughter.

A year or two after Squashy died, Dad decided that he'd demolish that row of pheasant enclosures and instead, put in a rose bed. This was duly done, looked very nice and improved the whole aspect of the playground. However, Dad being Dad, there had to be something different about the rose bed and it appeared in the shape of a 'Beast'. Dad bought a very large stone statue of a heraldic beast holding a shield and it was to be mounted on some stone slabs in the middle of the rose garden.

The Beast was one of several that had adorned the top of Manchester Assize Courts. These courts had been badly damaged by bombing during the war, and during the post war demolition process, several of these heraldic symbols had been saved and had finished up in a stonemason's yard from which Dad bought it. It was big, standing about 6 feet tall and it was heavy. When we tried to lift it with the front loader of the tractor, it started to lift the back wheels of the tractor off the ground despite there being a one-ton concrete block on the back! Assorted bodies balanced themselves on the back of the tractor and concrete block (*who mentioned "Health and Safety"!*) and equilibrium was restored. The Beast was then lowered onto its new plinth and was now located exactly where Squashy's cage had been.

We thought that our Beast may have been a famous heraldic Beast so made an enquiry of the College of Heralds. They didn't have a record of an animal like it, so it was probably simply a decorative piece dreamed up by the architect and stonemasons to adorn the frontage of the Assize Courts. Certainly, the shield that it's holding is part of the coat of arms of Manchester City Council.

On a much smaller scale than the Beast were the cats and dogs around the farm, and they were involved in one or two splendid incidents. The cats were ordinary moggies who kept the mouse and rat population under control though there was apparently one memorable cat that I was apparently associated with although I was too young to remember it. This was Ginger who was an elderly bad-tempered tomcat. If you put your hand down to stroke Ginger, you'd get it back dripping blood. But for some reason Ginger apparently liked me and allowed two-year-old me to pick him up and drape him over my arm and then wander round with both his front and back feet dragging on the floor. Naturally I don't remember any of this but the rest of the family with scratched hands and arms certainly did.

The type of dogs that we had changed from working collies like old Tip to things like Mastiffs and the big Standard Poodles. These latter were favoured by Mum because they didn't moult though they had to be trimmed every three months. I can just about remember that when I was very young, we also had Borzoi and Irish Wolfhounds. Apparently, we also had a Tibetan Mastiff, but the big dog I particularly remember was the big English Mastiff called Punch.

Punch was a lovely sweet-tempered dog. He was about the size of a Shetland pony and spent much of his day snoozing under the kitchen table. If someone came to door, Punch would get to his feet and head for the door, taking the kitchen table with him on his back! If it was meal time and doorbell rang, we all grabbed the table and lifted it up a bit before our dinner sped across the kitchen. He had a wonderful deep bark which he set off when someone rang the doorbell. We'd open the door and, if it was someone who was new to the farm, they'd ask if was safe because of the dog. Punch would push his way outside and proceed to give the visitor a good licking just to show how fierce he was. He was vastly entertaining whenever someone came to the front door. The front hall was entirely tiled but there was a rug half way down it. Someone knocking on the front door would bring Punch to his feet and he'd gallop from the kitchen into the hall. As he approached the front door at speed, he'd put the brakes on but by now he was on the rug. Punch and the rug would slide the last few feet and he'd hit the front door with an almighty thud. He'd do it every time. He never learned. A lovely natured dog but not the sharpest tool in the box.

The Standard Poodles were different again - very intelligent dogs. Jester caused us most amusement because he liked to travel. He'd sometimes accompany one of us on the bus, so he knew how the system worked. What he would do is wander off from the farm on his own and head for the nearest bus stop. He'd then sit quietly at the end of the queue and everyone thought he was with someone else. When the bus arrived, he'd get on and the conductor assumed he was with one of the passengers. He'd go upstairs and sit on a seat at the front of the bus so that he could have good view and then stay on until the bus stopped at the terminus. The conductor would find him upstairs as he finished his shift and then he'd get our phone number off Jester's collar. Next thing there'd be a phone call to the farm saying:

"Mr Bailey. Your dog's been riding on the bus again. Can you come to the terminus and collect him?"

What a dog!

Jester, the bus riding dog in front of Park Brow farmhouse

Chapter Eleven
Delivering Kellogg's Grains

I mentioned earlier how Kellogg's got the grains ready for collection by piping it into a tall hopper that we could back our trucks underneath and let the grains drop into the truck by releasing a sliding shutter. The grains had some odd properties though they normally had the consistency of slightly sloppy porridge. They were moved from the factory to the hopper by a long screw auger because one of the quirks of grains was that they froze into an almost solid lump if subjected to pressure, so pumping them was out. Which didn't help us with unloading. This was normally done by the driver and his mate climbing into the back of the truck wearing wellies and shovelling the stuff out into whatever receptacle (often an old pig sty) was at the receiving farm. This was done using specially shaped, aluminium shovels with handles so long that it was possibly to shovel the grains from all four corners of the back of the truck without moving from the centre of it. Once you got into the rhythm of it, it was surprising how fast you could empty a truck.

Kellogg's washed down their malting floor with boiling water, so the grains were often very hot. If you got a hot one to unload, you could only stand in the grains for a few minutes at a time while your feet were getting boiled in your wellies before leaping out to cool down. Sometimes the staff at Kellogg's were a little too enthusiastic when they were washing down and what came out of the hopper was liquid slop, highly unstable in the back of an open lorry and great care had to be exercised when driving, as a sudden stop could mean it sloshing forward and spilling on the road and even passers-by.

Dad always delighted in telling us the tale of how he'd got 'a sloppy one' on board one his earliest trucks and he'd pulled up very slowly and carefully at some traffic lights. There was a local bobby stood by the lights and, observing Dad's slow braking, he told him that he wasn't satisfied that the brakes on the truck were any good and that he intended to give him a braking test. In vain Dad explained that he was just being cautious. The bobby wouldn't listen and said that he was going to pedal up the road a short distance, get off his bike and then step out into the road with his hand up as Dad approached. It happened exactly like that except that Dad; knowing his brakes were good, left it a little bit late and then stamped on the brakes. A wave of grains sloshed down the back of the truck and went flying over the roof of the cab all over the copper. Dad said, "I think you'll agree there's nothing wrong with those brakes Officer" and drove off with a cheery wave. He fully expected to get a summons for an unsafe load but never did. Presumably the bobby didn't want to admit what had happened because of the ribbing that he'd get from his mates at the station.

Dad employed two or three regular drivers for delivering grains and of course he and my brother Bob drove when necessary as did Oliver and I when we were old enough. Laurie Yeo, one of the regular drivers, told a similar tale of being cut up by an open sports car when on the Chester Road and having to brake suddenly when it too had braked quickly. The same thing happened as with the bobby, only this time it was the back of the sports car got filled with grains. At the age of seventeen, I went out with Laurie and drove every day of the school holidays on L Plates to get driving experience before taking my driving test. For some reason Laurie hated cats. If we were driving through the suburbs of Chorlton and Stretford and he spotted a cat snoozing on a wall, he'd wait until we were almost level with it then smack the flat of his hand on the door panel of the truck, so it made a loud crack and the poor moggy would be shocked awake and race away.

The trucks that we drove were mostly Albions. They were painted a very smart bright green with gold lettering on the doors proclaiming to the world that they belonged to:

Leonard Bailey
Farmer and Farmers Merchant

The cabs all had a head board mounted above the windscreen which was painted with Leonard Bailey in large letters, so you'd be in no doubt about who had nearly run you over!

A preserved Albion Chieftain seen in 2005

Dad had started with an ex-WD Bedford and then had a Fordson before buying his first Albion which was probably a flat fronted Chieftain model. We had a procession of these, all petrol engined, and they were very reliable, but you had to concentrate to drive them. There was no synchromesh on the gear-boxes so your gear changes had to be very precisely timed to avoid hideous grinding noises. The steering was very heavy, but the brakes were good, and they were nice and snug in cold weather with the engine sat between driver and mate. Dad later bought a Diesel engined version and this was a real pig to drive. For starters, it was governed to not exceed 40 mph which was a pain after you'd delivered a load and wanted to get back quickly. Also, it had a very heavy flywheel so that it increased and decreased engine revs very slowly. This was a real curse when you wanted to double de-clutch to change gear, especially on a hill when you wanted to be in the next gear a.s.a.p.

The farms we delivered to mostly wanted their grains dropped into brick built open pits but some of them wanted the grains delivering into their cowsheds or milking parlours and this involved pulling up the truck alongside an opening in the cow shed wall and then we shovelled the grains through the hole, requiring great concentration. As Kellogg's expanded, their production of grains increased, and we were having to do more loads per day to keep the factory's hopper empty. And unloading by shovel was time consuming. This was the sting in the tail of the original contract with them. If we didn't keep the hopper cleared, we'd lose the contract. My brother Bob came up with the solution and this was to persuade the farmers to build pits for their grains so that we could use tipper lorries and drop the grains straight into the pits in a few minutes. Persuading the farmers was done by offering to subsidise the cost of building their new pits and most went along with it. So, we ordered our first tipping truck, and this came with a handsome aluminium body that was a bit like a storage tank in that its top was covered in with just a small hole in the centre for loading. This was a revelation as we'd no longer got the old problem of grains spilling out if we'd got 'a wet one' and, with the speedy unloading by tipping, a single driver could now do five or six loads a day instead of the 3 per day that was the previous max. And the drivers weren't coming home knackered after spending a day shovelling up to fifteen tons of grains. The only very slight downside was the fact that you had to reverse very accurately under the hopper to line up the aperture on the top of your truck with the bottom of the hopper.

We did have a bit of a problem in summer because summer was when more breakfast cereal was being sold and so we had more grains to shift. But summer is the time when farmers have their cattle out to grass and so they're using less animal food. Including grains. Dad got round this by offering some farmers very cheap loads of grains in the summer for storage. The farmers would dig out pits in their fields and we'd tip loads of grains onto them until they were full. If you kept the rain off the pits, the grains on the top would dry to a hard crust and seal in the bulk of the grains beneath. Come the winter, the farmer would break open the crust and dig out the good grains beneath.

There was one other aspect of keeping the hopper clear of grains and this was when Kellogg's were increasing production and running night shifts, so they were turning out grains twenty-four hours a day. Many's the time we were woken at two or three o'clock in the morning by a supervisor at Kellogg's ringing us up to say that the hopper was nearly full, and they wanted to drop another load into it in an hour or so.

All able-bodied family members would dress hurriedly and each leap into a truck to race down to the factory to fill it up. Once we'd loaded three or four trucks, we knew we'd got some breathing space and next morning the drivers would be told that their trucks were already loaded and to get out and deliver them as soon as possible then go back to the factory to re-load.

As the years went by, we noticed that many of our farmers were starting to use specialised packaged animal feeds from the like of Spillers or BOCM, especially if they were doing poultry farming as well as cattle. So, Dad started to offer to supply BOCM feeds for poultry, pigs and cattle and many of our farmers took him up. For this, we had to use flatbed trucks with side boards to contain the sacks of meal. This allowed us to recycle the old trucks of this type that we'd originally used to carry grains before we bought the tippers. Orders were phoned through to BOCM's mill in Trafford Park Docks and we'd go down with a lorry and wait beside a sloping chute for the big sacks each weighing one hundredweight to come whistling down. It's very hard work humping round hundredweight hessian sacks, so we were delighted when they got new packaging machines and started turning the products out in half hundredweight paper sacks. These were a delight to handle and stacked easily. It was this business of supplying BOCM feeds that kept the family business going as the grains trade declined.

Chapter Twelve

Dabbling in Politics and The Intervention of Private Eye!

The Tower Field was so named because there had been a stone-built tower half way along it that contained pumps, as it was part of the water distribution system for Manchester. The tower got demolished by a bomb in the war and was replaced by what can only be described as a rather large crude steel shed to house electric pumps. The field itself was a long narrow strip of land that we rented, and it was only a couple of hundred yards away from the farm and just over the brow of the railway bridge on St Werburgh's Road. It was about quarter of a mile long but only about 30 yards wide for most of its length, though it opened out quite a bit at the far end where it butted up to Wilbraham Road, one of the two main roads that crossed in the middle of Chorlton. It was in this wide area that Paulo's Circus had been held in 1940. This area was also used a couple of times for Conservative Summer fêtes The Tories were on a bit of a roll in the 1950s and did things like organising summer Fêtes to raise money for the party and this wide bit of the Tower Field got used because it was pretty close to the centre of Chorlton. At one of these fêtes, we children from the farm were tasked with managing a Zoo Tent which was populated with lots of Robert Jackson's animals. Somewhere there exists a photo of my sister Susan with a fair-sized python hanging round her neck at this event.

At the 1951 General Election, Florence Horsbrugh, later Baroness Horsbrugh, became surprisingly the Conservative MP for the constituency of Moss Side, which included Chorlton. The idea of a Conservative being MP for a place like Moss Side sounds ridiculous now, but it was a very different place in the 1950s. She became Minister of Education and was the first woman ever to do so in a Conservative Government. When she moved up to the House of Lords, she was replaced by James Watts (whose aunt was Agatha Christie) but he died suddenly in 1961 and a replacement was sought. As was usual, Conservative Central Office recommended people who they'd like to see get adopted and their choice was one Norman St John-Stevas of later great renown. Apparently, the local Selection Committee thought he was 'too clever by half' and appointed a meat and two veg type who would be acceptable to the more robust local populace.

It was at the beginning of Florence Horsbrugh's time that both my parents began to get interested in politics. We think that these Conservative fêtes played a part in the process and they were probably also influenced by one of their old friends. This was Robert Rodgers – always known as Bob – who was the very charismatic owner of a chain of florist's shops around Manchester and also a Tory councillor. He was renowned for always being very smartly turned out, wearing a carnation in his buttonhole and smoking cigarettes in a long holder. It was almost certainly Bob Rodgers who came up with the idea of approaching Dad to see if they could use his field for a fête. It was not long after this that Dad was asked to put up for election as a councillor for the Alexandra Park ward of the Moss Side constituency.

The family got its first taste of what electioneering was all about and how the Tory party's election machine worked. Firstly, all of us children helped with the preparation of polling cards and then their delivery to every house in the ward. The older children got to help out with canvassing of people to find out who would vote for Dad and to mark up their names on copies of the Electoral Register. On Polling Day, we younger ones got posted to wait outside the polling stations to collect the polling cards from people who had just voted and these were then rushed back every hour on our bikes to committee rooms (usually someone's front room) where they were ticked off on the copies of the Electoral Register so that we could see which of those who said that they would vote for Dad had actually done so. Then after about five o'clock, people were sent out to knock on the doors of those who had said that they'd vote for Dad to remind them of their promise and that the Polling Stations closed at nine o'clock. Sometimes they would be offered a lift to their Polling Station. It was a pretty slick operation and with good candidates, it delivered the results. In our case, Dad was pretty well known in the area and so was elected with a decent majority and we thought that we could relax for the next three years until he was up for re-election.

Wrong!

Once the local Tory party had found some willing workers (i.e.us) they were round asking us to help out next year as well. In those days, there were three Councillors for each ward and each one came up for re-election once every three years. So, we got asked to help with the election process next year for another candidate for Alexandra Park Ward. It became an annual task because Mum had become a party activist initially to support Dad but then became a regular Tory committee member and so she marshalled the family forces as well as getting friends involved. She really enjoyed it and became quite a mover and shaker behind the scenes in the Tory party and was eventually awarded an MBE for her efforts. Going to her presentation was the one and only time I went inside Buckingham Palace and we came home on the then famous Midland Pullman train enjoying a First-Class dining experience on the way. This was one of the first diesel super trains so was nicely streamlined and painted a very beautiful bright blue to distinguish it from bread and butter trains. It operated between Manchester and London and was all First Class

There was an entertaining incident on the train when dinner was served as the waiter asked what vegetables each of us wanted with our meal. I said 'peas' and there was a stunned silence round the table. As a small boy I'd hated peas and many a mealtime at the farm was a battle of wills between my parents and me to get me to eat peas. Hence the stunned silence. However, in the intervening years I had gone away to boarding school and there, you ate what you were given or starved. So, I acquired a tolerance, if not a liking for peas. When we got home from the palace, my parents told the rest of the family what I'd done and after their first disbelief, my brothers and sisters ragged me about for years afterwards. I didn't mind. I'd been to Buckingham Palace and ridden on the Midland Pullman. So there!

Dad was very committed to improving Manchester and was a popular councillor as he did a lot to help people in his ward regardless of their party affinity. Because of this, and his integrity in dealing with things entirely for the good of Manchester and its people, he was popular with the Labour Councillors as well. He kept getting elected with big majorities and eventually, the local Tory party asked him to become an Alderman, which meant that he was now a permanent member of the City Council

Hurray from us. A reduction in electioneering.

Like all councillors and aldermen, he served on a number of committees, and I know he particularly enjoyed his time with the Parks Committee and another committee that represented the City Council on Manchester University's management board. The University approved of him so much that they asked him to continue to serve on one their management committees after he'd finished with the City Council and later still, they awarded him an Honorary Degree as an MA. He was very proud of that. He also served on the Markets Committee and later became its Chairman. It was here that fate, or rather some aggrieved senior Tories, struck him down and ended his political career.

It all started when the Market Traders at Manchester's wholesale markets (think Smithfield and Covent Garden Markets rolled into one) needed to expand and asked the City Council to find them a new site. This was done, but there then followed some remarkable skulduggery as senior Tories tried to line their own pockets on the back of the New Market project. Private Eye magazine found out about the sordid business and told the story in the article that they published in April 1971 under the headline:

Won't you go home, Len Bailey.

And started with the memorable line: *'Amazing scenes are reported from Manchester Corporation...'*

What follows is taken from a copy of that article that I still have:

The complicated story started in 1965 when the Market Traders appointed a committee to liaise with the Council's

Markets Committee *(chaired by Dad)* to identify a site for a new market and to get funding for it. They found a suitable site at Openshaw in North Manchester and applied for Government grants for the project at a cost of £3.3m. However, in May 1967, the Conservatives took control of the Council and promptly removed the New Market project from the list of priorities. The market traders protested bitterly at the delay and did so for a couple of years, until in September 1969 they were approached by representatives of a company (we'll call it Co. A) proposing an alternative site for the new market. It turned out that one of the directors of this company was a senior member of the Conservative Party on the Council (we'll call him Mr A).

Co. A suggested that the market traders need not wait for the Council to grant the £3.3m, as instead they could put up a new, cheaper scheme, thus with lower rents, on a site that Co. A just happened to have acquired. This was an old factory near Old Trafford football ground. So, some of the traders went to view the site but it soon became clear that the scheme on this site would not be much cheaper, and the site suffered from industrial pollution, so would be completely unsuitable for the sale of fresh fruit and vegetables. The Traders Committee turned down Co. A's plan and renewed their demands for the Openshaw site.

The Council eventually agreed, and the necessary loan came through from the Ministry of Agriculture in April 1970, so work was planned to start early in 1971. Then in July 1970, Mr A personally approached some of the senior market traders and tried to interest them again in Co. A's alternative site, but he was again rebuffed.

On July 24th however, a planning application was submitted for a big, wholesale, cash-and-carry warehouse and a garage to be built on a site in Openshaw adjoining the one for the proposed new Wholesale Market. This was given Outline Approval on October 7th. This application was made by another company (Co. B) in which a director and company secretary was a leader of the Conservative Group (Mr B) on the Council. The market traders were rightly furious.

Still the Tories on the Council dithered, so in December, Dad's Market Committee appointed management consultants from Egham, Surrey to examine every aspect of the Openshaw project, especially the design and financial prospects, as at this stage, every month's delay cost the ratepayers £30,000 in loan charges.

The consultants' report of February 4th, 1971 commended in every way the suitability and viability of the Openshaw project but still the Conservative Group was not satisfied. A Conservative councillor (Mr C) argued that the report be sent back to the consultants for further consideration, and, suitably whipped, the Tory group approved this course of action. Then, Mr A and Mr B asked if they could go and talk to the consultants themselves. Dad, as chairman of the Market Committee refused to let them do so. At about the same time, the Council's planners had imposed a condition on the scheme proposed by Co. B that they could not sell goods in competition with the new Market. Co. B withdrew their application.

Meanwhile, the market traders committee heard about this latest delay caused by asking the consultants to reconsider their conclusions and wrote a scorching letter to the Town Clerk. As well as complaining at this latest delay after six years of design and planning, they noted that rents were set to rise by 25% because of the increased costs and that almost every other big city in the UK had already rebuilt their markets.

No less enraged were the consultants who replied brusquely that they had examined every aspect of the new Market project with the greatest possible care in their original report. They said that a further survey was unnecessary, and they had nothing to add.

This was enough for Dad. Without consulting the Conservative Group, he notified all members of the Market Committee that a special meeting would be held on 26th March to give the go-ahead to the Openshaw project.

The Tory leaders were furious and told Dad that his presence was required at a 'high level meeting' at the Conservative offices on 23rd March. Dad told them that he could not make that meeting. Then, the deputy chairman of the Conservative group called on Dad at home on the evening of 24th March to demand that he call off the special meeting. Dad refused.

At the special meeting of the Market Committee on 26th March, Dad revealed that the Openshaw development had been obstructed for several months. He also disclosed that Mr A had made an approach to the City Council's Director of Markets and made a further attempt to switch the project to Co. A's site. The Tories on the Market Committee who had not been made aware of what had been going on were stunned into silence. A Labour Alderman proposed that the Openshaw scheme be confirmed. Labour members and Dad voted for it, while the Tories abstained.

The matter then went to Finance Committee for approval on 30th March, and, again, Mr A and Mr B tried to get the project postponed. By now, other Tories had become aware of what had been happening and four of them voted with the seven Labour members to approve an immediate start to the Openshaw project. Four Tories voted against, including the Letter Men and their friend, Mr D.

The full City Council meeting confirmed the project on April 7th. However, the Letter Men wanted revenge, and Dad was summoned before the Tory Caucus to be disciplined for 'disloyalty to Conservatism'. This resulted in losing his place as Alderman and, thus, his career in politics, but he'd certainly gone out in style and with head held high. In a wry finale, the Labour Group on the Council offered him a place as one of their Aldermen, partly in recognition of his fight for what was right and partly because of his reputation as someone who worked hard for Manchester.

Dad thanked them for their kind offer but declined it.

How Private Eye got the inside story of all these shenanigans is a mystery. It certainly wasn't Dad and or any of his friends in the Tory party who were likely to be Private Eye readers. Whoever it was had known the full details of the story, so it was probably one of the senior members of the Market Traders committee. They made sure to uncover some sticky politics and give credit where credit was due.

Well done Dad.[1]

---

[1] (1971) Won't You Go Home, Len Bailey. *Private Eye Magazine,* (243), 20-21.

Chapter Thirteen
Transports of Delight

While we were growing up – remember there were five children – Dad had a series of large cars and the first I remember was a big, black Wolseley 21. Dad used to pack all the family in to take us on holiday to Lytham St Annes. On one memorable occasion, an overheating exhaust set the floor boards to smouldering. I think it was Susan who got warm first and raised the alarm and everyone piled out onto the road side while the fire extinguisher was used. Very exciting. Just the story for a "What we did on our holidays" essay when back at school!

That was followed by a massive Rolls-Royce Phantom II with very handsome Sedanca de Ville bodywork. This was also black and the roof over the rear compartment was covered in leathercloth and had large frames on either side so that it looked like the rear compartment had a hood over that could be folded back. It didn't. It was just a style thing. There were two huge headlights plus another spotlight mounted in front of the radiator and another movable spotlight mounted beside the driver's door. There were big spare wheel covers mounted on each wing and the whole thing just oozed class on the outside while internally there was a glass screen between the driver and the passengers that could be wound down. Needless to say, inside there was a dozen cows worth of leather and the rain forests had not been spared to provide all the mahogany. There was even a cocktail cabinet in the back as well as a radio – very rare in a 1930s car. Dad told us that it had once belonged to King Edward VIII, but nobody believed him, and Buckingham Palace certainly wasn't in the log book.

We found out many years later that this story about Edward VIII, that he'd been told by the car salesman, was surprisingly not far off the truth. The car had actually belonged to the Brownlow family of Belton House in Lincolnshire. Brownlow was Edward VIII's Equerry and had been a close personal friend of the King when he was Prince of Wales. So, Brownlow was heavily involved in the Abdication crisis and Edward VIII spent a lot of time at Belton over the years. So, he would certainly have been driven round in this car and may possibly have driven it himself. This wonderful monster is believed to have survived and to be somewhere in North America.

We used to go as family in this massive beast to visit my Uncle Will who now lived in North Wales just north of Barmouth. Only years later did we discover an odd connection between the old Rolls and Uncle Will. Uncle Will had served in the Machine Gun Corps in the First World War and he, like all the Corps, had been trained at Belton House near Grantham. Which is where the Rolls had been first owned twenty years later.

Uncle Will had got room to put us all up because he bought a large sheep farm and with it came an impressive 15th century hall so there were plenty of rooms. I remember that once we stopped for petrol at a little garage at Bontddu not far from Barmouth. The old Rolls only did about 12 miles to the gallon, so petrol stops were frequent. Dad pulled up in front of the one and only petrol pump and asked the attendant for 20 gallons. I'll never forget the look of utter dismay on his face when Dad said that.

"This is going to take some time" he said. "Why don't you all go over to the shop and have an ice cream while I get started".

Somewhat puzzled, we left the car but stood outside the shop eating our ice creams. As we watched the attendant putting petrol in the car, we suddenly realised that we were looking at what had to be one of the earliest petrol pumps ever made. It was tall, and the hose snaked down from just below two large glass jars at the top of the pump about 6 feet from the ground. The attendant rocked a lever backwards and forwards and petrol steadily filled one of the glass jars. When it was full, he turned another lever so that the second jar started filling as he pumped away and at the same time, the first jar started emptying by gravity through the hose and into the car. So, the poor old guy had to do this twenty times and it took about quarter of an hour. No wonder he looked so dismayed.

In the early post war years, it was almost impossible to buy new cars as the British motor manufacturers were told by the Government to export most of what they produced in order to earn foreign currency. Second hand pre-war cars were therefore in great demand and cars from quality manufacturers were sought out as they would keep going when the pre-war Fords, Austins and Morrises had given up the ghost. This is what led Dad to buy the Rolls and the idea caught on. It wasn't unusual in those days to see several Rolls Royces at the farm, because when there was a family gathering there would be three or four. Uncle Will, Uncle Seymour, Les Davenport and Bob Rodgers (family friends) all had them.

Eventually the Phantom had a serious engine problem and it was succeeded by a Mark VI Bentley, which had the mechanical servo brakes favoured by Rolls Royce. However, one night they failed to stop the car and it entered the infamous East Lancs Road at speed to Dad's great shock and he lost all confidence in it. It was quickly replaced by 3.4 Mk2 Jaguars of the Inspector Morse sort.

The first of these Jags had the wonderful registration number of CUT 4 and when I was out and about in it in my late teens, that was often the state of the passengers. It was a wonderful looker with a very distinctive metallic bronze paint job that looked like gold and it also had chrome spoked wire wheels. It was known as the Ginger Jag. If you turned up at a party on your own in it, you could guarantee that you'd be leaving with a pretty girl in the passenger seat. The second Jag was again a 3.4 model but was a soberer maroon colour and was in much better order mechanically so lasted for many years being taken over by Bob as his daily driver.

After the old Mark VI, Dad always hankered after a new Bentley and while it was on order, he had one of the first Silver Shadow Rolls Royces, an ex-demonstrator, that was beset with teething problems and the worst of these was the way it scrubbed tyres. Because the damn thing was so heavy, they had used a tyre developed for Cadillacs, but they screwed up the design of the independent suspension – that we learnt thirty years later at the Royal show when the sales technician freely admitted it. In fact, things were so bad that when it went for service at Rolls Royce in Crewe, they used to dread the arrival of Dad with the list of things that needed fixing but at least when he took delivery of its Bentley replacement it was a bit better but far from perfect. A few years later, he traded up to a new Silver Shadow, but this was properly sorted, and he was very happy with it for years.

When Mum decided it was time she learned to drive, Dad bought her an old pre-war Ford Model Y named 'Claude the Ford.' She had a licence from before the war but wasn't at all confident, so she had driving lessons first with Dad. Dad didn't last long as an instructor because he had the habit of raising his hat at cyclists that she passed on the grounds that they didn't know what a narrow escape from death they had just had. Mother was not amused. Bob took over and I sometimes sat with him as Mum struggled with the old Ford's vague steering, iffy brakes and a 3-speed gearbox with no synchromesh on 1st gear. We used to call these driving lessons "Much Grinding in the Marsh" after the then popular radio programme "*Much Binding in the Marsh*".

Mum battled valiantly with Claude but wanted something easier to drive than the old Model Y, so she tried out a newer Ford Popular that a local lady was selling. It was still a 'Sit up and beg' model so it wasn't a big transition from the original Ford, and she was happy with it for a few years until she traded up to a Ford Anglia. This was the model with the reverse rake to the rear window as seen flying in the Harry Potter films. For quite a while this car suffered from a terrible vibration at speeds between 30 and 40 mph that no-one at the Ford dealers seemed to know how to cure. Someone suggested that the wheels could need balancing though at the time, this was usually only an issue with performance cars. A quick visit to a tyre dealers and, with freshly balanced front wheels, the problem vanished. After a few years of the Anglia, she had a Vanden Plas Princess 1100. Very smart and luxurious for such a small car. Once Oliver and I were of driving age, we were allowed to borrow all of Mum's cars to go out in the evenings. I nearly trashed the Anglia one night when chasing friends round the back lanes of Cheshire and losing it on a sharp bend. I did a complete one-eighty and finished up stopped, facing the wrong way just inches from a high bank. Phew! I didn't let on about that one. Mum while out with friends once broke down on the little Vanden Plas and rang in to the farm for rescue. While she was waiting for someone to arrive, the police spotted 4 ladies clearly with a problem and stopped to offer assistance. They were told that help was on its way, but they still kept driving past regularly to check that all was well until they were sure that they'd been properly taken care of. I'm afraid I can't see such a thing happening today.

Other interesting vehicles were owned by Bob who had a couple of pre-war MG's until he got married. The first one was a J2 model and was special in that it had been modified for racing and had a streamlined cowl over the radiator plus extra streamlining around the cockpit. If you look at photos of cars racing at Brooklands in the 30s, you'll see something similar being used by the serious contenders. The next one was a K type and was either a K1 or a K2 and not the supercharged (and very valuable) K3 model. This had a 6-cylinder engine and a voracious appetite for clutches! Practically every other weekend Bob was underneath it, changing the clutch. It was a family joke that he was asked if it was its week for running! Bob's friend Trevor also had MG's and the two of them were always tinkering and trying to get more speed out of them.

They had both installed oversized rear wheels to gain some extra speed and one day, when Trevor had a puncture, inevitably I suppose, in a rear tyre, he called Bob to bring him a spare. While he waited, Trevor who was smartly dressed in sports jacket and peaked cap, was being chaffed by a group of people from another car and Bob somehow divined what was happening and as he drove up in Dad's Phantom II, he tootled the four-note horn. The group who were harassing Trevor were suitably abashed when Bob got out of the Rolls, touched his forelock and addressed Trevor as "Your Lordship", leaving the scoffers with their tails between their legs. Another small victory for the forces of righteousness.

Once when Bob was arguing about cars over a family meal, he stated flatly that Dad, a gentleman of some corpulence, couldn't even fit in let alone drive one of MG's. Father said nothing but later that day, when Bob had gone on some errand

Oliver was called outside to find my father ensconced in said MG but with one difficulty, he couldn't start it. Oliver showed him where the foot operated starter switch was and was invited to accompany him in a drive down the road. They didn't go far but Robert's face was a picture when they drove back into the yard.

I'd been driving the farm's Ferguson tractor, the famous little grey Fergie, since I was about thirteen and was driving it round the streets by the age of fifteen to deliver loads of manure to allotment holders. I took my tractor test as soon as I was sixteen to make it legal. Then when I was seventeen, I had a few driving lessons but then failed my driving test as I didn't have enough 'road sense' according to the examiner. Dad promptly stuck some L plates on one of the trucks and sent me out to work driving with Laurie. Laurie was happy with this as he'd got an assistant to help him shovel grains off and he could relax (more or less) while I battled with the weighty steering and crash gear-box of the old Albion. A few weeks of that and I passed my test next time. You learned a lot of road sense driving with a sloppy load of grains behind you, requiring you to anticipate carefully what the other traffic around you was doing if you weren't to slop a lot onto the road.

My first personal transport was a Vespa scooter. This was a really early one, made under licence by Douglas, and was completely gutless. Anything over 30mph was only achievable either downhill or with a following wind. Preferably both! This being the time of Mods and Rockers, I dolled it up with wing mirrors and a tall aerial with pennants with a little light on the top but nothing I could do would make it go any faster. It had to go. One night at a party at a friend's house near Wilmslow, I spotted a car parked up in the garden looking lost and lonely. I asked the host what it was, and he told me that it was an old Talbot 10 Drophead Coupe, but it hadn't run for a few years. It had an attractive body shape and wind-up windows to keep the weather out. Silvery wire wheels, louvres all along the bonnet and two big headlights made it look very sporty and the body didn't seem to be in too bad condition. I agreed to buy it from him for £2.50p (that was 50 shillings in those days).

Next day I casually suggested at mealtime that I'd been offered quite a nice car for 50 shillings and Dad's immediate reaction was to say, "You're not bringing that load of old junk round here!" Dad had good reason for saying this as I'd got involved in a scheme only twelve months previously in which three friends and I had jointly purchased an old Daimler with the idea of getting it mobile enough for us to embark in a journey to Italy in it. The Daimler was parked up under a shed in the Stackyard and we tinkered with it to get it mobile. We succeeded in getting the engine running and were well pleased with its smooth running until there was a mighty bang and a clatter from the front and we found that it had thrown a connecting rod through the block. So that was the end of that, and it was towed away to a scrap yard.

Amusingly, about a year later the three friends and one other actually managed to set out for Italy in two ratty old cars and nearly made it. One of the cars expired terminally on an Alpine pass and, waiting until no-one was about, they simply shoved it over the side to crash into the void below and then carried on in the surviving old Rover.

Meanwhile, it was time for some cunning if I was to get the Talbot to somewhere that I could work on it and ideally, that meant home.

We'd got a storage area with a loft above across the Yard and this was filled with all sorts of junk and no-one ever went in. If I could move the junk to the loft, then I'd have a space to keep the Talbot and work on it with only a small chance of discovery. Working when no-one was about, I got the space cleared then looked for a suitable time when Dad and Mum would be out. I'd got a group of friends on stand-by to help tow the Talbot and I'd been to it a couple of times to check that the wheels were rolling freely and that it had brakes. The latter was a dismal failure as a brake worked on one rear wheel if you hauled on the hand brake but that was all. I discussed it with the lads we decided that we'd risk it by towing very slowly. On the chosen day, four of them appeared to collect me in Nelson's father's Humber Hawk which we thought would have enough grunt for the job.

We got the Talbot onto the road and hitched up to the tow-rope easily enough and then set off. Nelson was driving slowly in the Humber and by hauling on the handbrake, I could slow just enough to avoid running into the back of it when he stopped at junctions. We were using back roads but had completely forgotten that one of them had a steepish hill on it. I was steering happily and two of the guys were watching out of the rear window of the Humber when I saw one them wave his arms and he was clearly shouting to Nelson in the driving seat that I was catching them up down the hill. Rather rapidly. And the single brake was having little effect. And the tow-rope had now got a lot of slack in it. I could see the look of terror in the faces of my friends in the back of the Humber as they saw a brakeless me bearing down on them and they were clearly shouting warnings to Nelson in the driving seat. Nelson panicked and put his foot down to accelerate clear but the tow-rope had gone under the front wheels of the Talbot and so snapped with a terrific twang as Nelson pulled away. I was now cast adrift and coasting down this hill with little chance of stopping at the bottom where the road stared to rise again. The others in the Humber were keeping well clear as I picked up speed then started to go up the other side. I was thinking ahead far enough to realise that when the Talbot ran out of momentum, it would stop and then run back down again, and the others wouldn't be able to get near enough to help by chocking a wheel. A light bulb moment! As the car stopped, I put it in 1st gear and she stayed still. While I wiped the sweat off my brow, the others backed the Humber up to me, re-attached the tow-rope and much chastened, we set off very carefully. Getting it into the storage area was comparatively simple and the doors were closed, and I kept away for a few days only starting to work on it when Dad wasn't about.

Mum being around the house for much of the day soon spotted me disappearing into the shed and came across to see what was happening. By this time, I'd got the engine running and done a tidy up, so she thought it looked quite smart and was a reasonable project. I told her I'd have to do quite a lot to the brakes and she kindly coughed up for new brake cables and linings. She must have told Dad what was afoot, but he diplomatically didn't go poking around and didn't mention it until it was almost ready to be rolled out. By this time, as well as a thorough overhaul, I'd re-wired it, fitted a nearly new hood and welded patches in to the corroded wings and running boards. After painting the repaired areas, the whole car looked very smart indeed. And it ran surprisingly well passing its MOT test with ease.

It belied its sporty looks because under the skin it was a 1930s Hillman Minx which meant it was very easy to find spares for but wasn't a flyer. I had a lot of fun in it. It did have an Achilles heel in the shape of the back axle. This used to let go of its half shaft so that as you went round a corner, the half shaft with wheel still attached leapt out sideways so the car was now 2 feet wider but not going anywhere. Exciting, but hardly the extending tyre cutter of James Bond's DB5. After one such incident we had to change the rear wheel bearing in the car park of the Rising Sun in Stockport. Once I'd isolated the cause of this peculiar habit and done a permanent fix it was absolutely fine. As you can see from the picture. It was quite an attractive looking car and I enjoyed owning it.

A Talbot 10 Drop Head Coupe similar to mine

The Talbot was followed by a very quick TVR Grantura that had been severely breathed on by Mangoletsi's who were one of the top tuners in the region. Under the bonnet it seemed to be all carburettors and an exhaust system that resembled a basket of writhing snakes. Its highly modified Ford engine caused some confusion later on as TVR at Blackpool had switched to using MGB engines and when they had repaired the bodywork, they put on the plug leads in MGB sequence instead of Ford causing serious misfiring. It was taken to a guy who prepared racing Minis and he couldn't solve it but offered to re tune it for free if we ever solved the problem. Bob had a flash of inspiration, looked at Mum's Ford Anglia, swapped over two plug leads and it roared into life. When the car was taken back for its tune up said expert mechanic accused us of lying and then swore us to silence once it was shown we were right – he did do the tune up though.

Oliver had a pretty, black MGA that got written off after he hit black ice at 60 mph and rolled it into a field one winter night. Shame. It was a nice car and I took out my wife-to-be on our first date in it. The MGA was succeeded by a speedy Triumph Vitesse 2 Litre. This was memorably crashed by Bob after he had picked it up from the dealers and before Oliver had even seen it, as its vivid acceleration caught Bob by surprise. Like Queen Victoria, Oliver was not amused.

Years later in another famous incident a friend came round to take Oliver and his wife out to dinner and this guy Mike rolled up in his Lotus Elan feeling very chipper. That lasted only a couple of minutes as Dad swept into the Yard driving his Rolls, took one look at Mike's pride and joy and said, "What do you wear on the other foot, son?" Mike dined out on that story for years.

Of course, a farm needed a pickup truck for small loads and the first was a Standard Vanguard that unladen was surprisingly fast. I used to use this as my transport before the Talbot was ready, but I managed to write it off when spinning off on a corner near Handforth on a wet night. Bob was not at all amused by this as he was fond of the Vanguard, but he cheered up when we acquired a long wheelbase Series 2 Land Rover. Both Oliver and I liked the Land Rover and it was good for visiting pubs with friends. These pub visits could get a bit hairy as a gang of us raced from one pub to another and most of us had a prang at some time, but they were slow speed affairs, and no-one got hurt. An entertaining one was when David clipped the verge and rolled his little Fiat 600 at the top of a hill near Mottram St Andrew and slid all the way down on its roof to the great alarm of a car coming the other way. Those of us following stopped and, having checked that no-one was hurt, rolled the Fiat back on to its wheels and five minutes later they were back on their way.

One odd 'motoring' event occurred when Bob had the bright idea of building a go-kart. We had an old Villiers engine lying about that had come off some old farm machinery; we had spare wheelbarrow wheels and lots of scrap steel plus a gas welding kit. Why not? So, the three of us put together this monstrosity which looked like it been dreamt up for '*Scrapheap Challenge*'. It also had brakes that George Stephenson would have disapproved of. We fired it up and ran it round the yard and found that fortunately, it wouldn't go any faster than 10 miles an hour. We needed a bigger stage to play on so took it across the road from the farm onto Cavendish Road. This was a public road but had just six houses on one side and a wide unpaved centre that was covered in packed cinders. We ran the mad contraption round and round spraying up cinders like speedway riders and missed seeing a policeman come past! He stopped, looked at us and said: "I ought to charge you lot with several traffic offences but you're clearly having so much fun that I'll let it go." Phew!

The three of us also had the idea of having a boat between us and the first was a half deck speed boat called Txibange (don't ask) with a trailer that could be towed by the Land Rover to the canal or the seaside. This was sold to a friend of Oliver's who lived near Newport Pagnell and one winter evening he and a friend drove there to deliver it. And Gerard Hoffnung could have scripted the journey. Half way down the M6 the trailer started to crab, and a check revealed that a wheel bearing was running hot, but they decided to press on only to realise things were getting worse, so the boat was loaded into the back of the Land Rover, so they could proceed down the Queen's highway. However, things did not get better, they got worse, much worse and just as they pulled onto the off ramp for a service station, the wheel finally came off and just like a cartoon, rolled past the vehicle. There was only one thing to do and so the trailer was loaded on top of both boat and Land Rover with the tow bar pointing over the cab like a gun barrel. And the journey was completed like that.

Ambition knows no bounds and a successor boat was purchased, larger and more impressive. For this a largish outboard motor was required. Bob found someone selling off brand new and unused engines that were now out of production so were cheap but had no warranty or manufacturer's back-up. Bob wanted to test out the engine to make sure it was OK, so he came up with the scheme of filling a large galvanised dustbin with water and putting the outboard in it clamped to the edge. The engine was started in neutral and run while we checked it was running smoothly and that the water pump was working. All was well, so we revved it up a bit and then Bob foolishly put it in gear so that the propeller was now turning. Not a good idea! This was a powerful outboard in a very confined location so 30 gallons of water blew straight up in the air and then down on the three of us. That's last time that was tried.

Giselle-17

    Inspired by our nautical activities, two chaps called Frank & Brian, who were now running the garage behind the farm, decided that they too should get a boat. The boat they got was given to them in settlement of an unpaid account. They were robbed.

    Possibly the ugliest boat ever to take to the water it was called Fred. Entirely timber built with an oddly shaped cabin on top and with a cranky old Ford engine, it looked awful. To jazz it up a bit, they painted it red, so naturally it became 'Red Fred'. They took the beast on a trailer down to the canal at the "Old Number 3" pub not far from Altrincham. Red Fred was dropped in the water and Frank and Brian got her running and chugged off for a maiden voyage. They left her moored up and went off home after a celebratory pint. However, being complete nautical novices, they hadn't realised that wood shrinks when it dries out and Red Fred had been out of the water and stored undercover for many years. Unseen, under the cabin floor she was filling up nicely and when they called back at the pub a couple of days later, only the cabin top was above water. There followed a splendid salvage operation which kept the drinkers at the pub amused for hours before Red Fred was hauled onto the bank, trailered away and never seen again.

Chapter Fourteen
Daily Stuff at The Farm

Mornings at the farm were always slightly surreal. The fire in the kitchen grate had been banked down the night before and Dad, first down, poked it into life, drew the dampers and soon had it built up and roaring away again. Meanwhile the kettle had boiled, tea had been mashed in a massive pot and this was placed in front of the grate to keep warm. As we came down to have breakfast, there was a steady procession of visitors arriving at the back door and being given mugs of tea. First in was usually the milkman who left his float outside and chatted for five minutes while he slurped his tea. He was usually joined by the drivers of the grains trucks who discussed their runs for the day with Dad or Bob and picked up their delivery tickets. Then there was one or two of the farm hands who wanted their brief for the day as well as their tea ration and finally the postman who got a nice break from his round as well as a mug of tea. There could be four or five people crowded round the kitchen doorway or overflowing into the scullery next door with cats and dogs dodging about underfoot. In the middle of all this, Miss Sheridan, the daily help arrived and also had a cup of tea before starting to clear away the breakfast things. Oliver and I got on with our breakfasts and tried to ignore the uproar and good-natured chaffing before grabbing our satchels and running off to catch the bus to school.

Things quietened down once the trucks had left. Cats and dogs got fed. The parrot and the canary got fed and Dad usually attended to the large tank of tropical fish that sat in the window. In those days, he had to constantly clean the water filter and the aerators and fiddle with the air pump, of which we had many different types, that were rarely trouble free for long. The farm hands got on with the business of feeding the pigs and mucking them out and then on to the chickens.

Dad had bought a chicken battery house and installed it in the Stackyard behind the Dutch barn on the site of our old woodpile. This was a state of the art set up for the 1950s as the hens were fed and cleaned out automatically and lived in three tiers. The bottom of the hens cages were made of wire mesh and underneath that was a long sheet of glass that ran the whole length of the battery. To attend to the hens, you first put a bag of chicken feed into each of three hoppers (at three different levels, one for each row of cages) then went round to the other side and did the same again as the cages were back to back. You then pressed a button and an electric motor operated a cable system to draw the hoppers slowly along the row of cages leaving an even spread of feed in the troughs that ran in front of the cages. At the same time that hoppers were running one way, scrapers that had started at the other end of the row were being pulled in the reverse direction to scrape the chicken muck off the long glass sheets. When they got to the end of their run, the scrapers dropped the muck into large trays and then set off back to the end as the hoppers also reversed. Whoever's job it was, then pulled out the trays of chicken muck and dumped them in a wheelbarrow to go on the midden. So far so easy.

Then it was time to collect the eggs and that was an unmechanised long slog. The wire mesh bases of the cages were set at a slight slope so the eggs when laid rolled forwards and were held by more mesh in front of each cage. When collecting, you set off with a small stack of the compressed cardboard egg trays held in one hand and just worked your way along the cages. Each tray held thirty eggs, so when the top tray was full, you lifted it away from the empty trays and put it on the ground and carried on until the next tray was full and so on. The top and middle rows weren't too bad to work along but you had to work crouched down to empty the bottom row. Then you went round again picking up the full trays from the floor and bringing them to be stacked in wooden crates at the front of the shed. Then you went round again picking up any eggs that you'd rejected because they were cracked or broken.

The boxes of eggs would be wheeled round to the yard and then all the trays were inspected to grade them for size and put any aside that needed washing. Graded full boxes were then locked shut and moved to a store on the far side of the yard to await collection by an egg packing company who called two or three times a week. We always kept back quite a few trays of eggs in the scullery and sold them at the door. This kept Miss Sheridan busy. The cracked eggs also came into the farm house and were used for cooking. All in all, it was quite a job keeping on top of the egg business.

We had some mad light relief with the eggs when Linda's husband Peter read in the *New Scientist* that eggs were structurally much stronger than they appeared. Not only were they structurally quite strong but because they had a yolk inside, if thrown onto grass, on landing the movement of the yolk acted as a shock absorber and prevented the egg from breaking. The offending article said this would even work if you threw an egg over a two-storey house to land on a lawn. This had to be tried. So, we went into the yard armed with half a dozen eggs and proceeded to hurl them over the roof of the house so that they'd land on the lawn. We then dashed round to the garden to check the results and three of the six eggs had indeed survived their flight. Two had cracked and shattered and another, thrown by Oliver, had missed the roof entirely and landed in the road. When we looked for it, we saw a bemused cyclist looking up the skies for the mystery bird that had just missed him when it laid an egg in flight! Dad was interested in the results but banned further trials as the failed eggsperiments would make a nasty mess of his lovely lawn.

Obviously, we were at school during the day but expected to help out on the farm at other times, so we helped looking after the pigs and the egg business both at Park Brow and Hough End. We also fed the ducks and Oliver got to feed the calves before he went to school which meant an early start for him.

We also got roped in to help the neighbours from time to time and the Greers across the road were regular clients as old Mrs Greer was always locking herself out. We got quite good at breaking in using a ladder and a first-floor window. We also once helped to rescue her daughter Florence from her car. She'd got a little three-wheeler Isetta that you had to open the whole front of the car to get in and out. It also had no reverse gear.

One day, she drove too far into her drive towards the garage and so found herself trapped as she couldn't open the front, nor could she go back! She opened a window and her yells for help were heard by her mother who came over the road to the farm to get help. We went over to drag the car back, much amused at Florrie's predicament.

When we got a bit bigger, we helped unloading trucks of pig and chicken feed and stacking them in the store and as mentioned earlier, we helped out on the midden loading muck onto the trailer by hand ready for delivery to the allotments. We were glad to see the end of that job when the farm acquired a front loader for the tractor though this led to another job as the midden needed a new concrete floor so that tractor wouldn't get bogged down. It also needed a new retaining wall at one side that Bob and Oliver built by heaving and straining to build using massive stone slabs. They put a sign up at the end of the yard to advertise their efforts. It read "Khufra and Cheops - Pyramid builders to the nobility".

Like most farms, we had a fair few rats in residence and these dug their burrows mostly under the buildings where the feed was stored which was also near the swill vats. Once in a while, a Rat Hunt was organised, and everyone took part, even the drivers. The entries to the rats' dens would be spotted and everyone gathered round holding large shovels and with dogs ready on leashes. There was also a supply of clods of earth and good-sized stones made ready. Dad and/or Bob would stand further back from the crowd ready with shot guns. Once everyone was ready, a large diameter hose pipe would be stuffed down the first hole and the water turned on. After a while, water would start to bubble out of another hole, and this was quickly blocked with a clod of earth with a stone stamped down to secure it. As the rats den filled up, we spotted more exits as the water bubbled out and then the rats started to emerge, swimming out on the flood only to get clobbered by flying shovels. Those that escaped the shovels were grabbed by the dogs and one little terrier called Jock was a very fine rat catcher. Very occasionally, one would get far enough away for the shotgun to be used safely but this wasn't often and the whole nest was usually wiped out by the shovels and dogs.

Other bits of daily life were different from the norm and shopping was another oddity. We had a newsagent, butchers and a grocers only quarter of a mile away 'over the bridge' but Mum and Dad only rarely used the grocers. This was because they wanted to use the grocers that they'd used when they were first married and living in Old Chorlton about a mile away. What used to happen was that the son of the family that owned the shop - the Whitakers – used to call at the farm once a week. He'd take a seat in the kitchen with Mum and, armed with a mug of tea, he'd go through recitation of all the goods that Mum might want. "Jams, jellies and Marmalades; Soaps, Sodas and Blues" is all I can remember of the recitation, but he finished up with a long list of dry goods and then he'd call round that evening to deliver it. Just like Ocado only 60 years ago.

With a large family to feed, Mum kept a well-stocked pantry and was happy to take advantage once the first frozen foods appeared. A freezer was required and naturally, these were rare beasts in the early 1950s, but Dad managed to magic up a Lyons Ice Cream freezer from a cinema that was closing. There were very few suppliers of frozen foods in those day of which Birds Eye was the best known but there were a few other new guys on the block including one now defunct company called Albatross which were stocked by our nearest grocer. Once when Dad was going over the bridge to get a bit of shopping for Mum, she called after him "And a large Albatross peas." Dad turned round and with an innocent look on his face asked, "Does it?"

Mum thought that Oliver and I needed more culture and so were told that we would be having piano lessons. This was not popular with either of us as of course the lessons had to happen outside school hours and so were taking up our time. And we were forced to practice in between lessons by Mum or our sisters. We mastered a few simple tunes but then this meant that we were 'shown off' and asked to perform in front of people who visited or, even worse, in other people's houses if they'd got a piano. Highly embarrassing. Oliver hated the whole business even more than me, and he had a particular way of showing it. We'd been given a little piece to learn which practised the use of chords with both hands. It was a gentle little piece called '*The Quiet Wood*' and I can remember the words to it from sixty years ago:

Softly the breeze
Is swaying the trees
To sing me to sleep
In the quiet wood.

Obviously meant to be played gently, Oliver would sit down at the piano and, with foot firmly on the loud pedal, would pound out the chords at full volume. Then do it again, And again. Until he was told to shut up, which was his excuse to end practice.

It was known as Oliver's Hymn of Hate.

Mum gave up on us and I don't think we were any great loss to the world of music – though somewhere I've got a clutch of certificates I earned from the College of Music. Perhaps that's where our daughter Gil gets her musical talent from.

There were however other cultural influences in our lives as Dad maintained a large library of books including a very good reference section. This came into play with Dad's regular Sunday Quizzes. As a family, we'd sit down for Sunday lunch and afterwards the radio would be on with such gems as '*Billy Cotton's Band Show*' or '*Take it From Here*'. But about every other Sunday, Dad would run a quiz to check what we'd learned and remembered. He have rounds of Geography, History, Literature and so on and ask each of us a question in turn and mark us with a tick or a cross on a piece of paper. The older three, Linda, Susan and Robert would often challenge what Dad had said was the right answer with much loud protesting that they were right, and Dad was wrong. The reference library in the bookcase beside the dining table was then consulted and it wasn't often that Dad was wrong. I now find that Dad's Sunday lunchtime training comes in very handy when I do pub quizzes.

Family arguments and events of the week were regular topics of conversation at these lunches and I well remember Bob being thoroughly out-argued by Dad over the matter of his chickens. In his late teens, Bob had decided that he'd make some extra cash for himself by raising some chickens from day-old chicks and then selling them on for eating at Christmas to customers who came to the door buying eggs. When most of them had been sold, Bob asked for his share of the proceeds. Dad said:

"Well let's start with the total sale value, but then you need to deduct my costs for providing their accommodation and providing their feed. Then there's the cost of electricity for heating and lighting the area. Plus, the costs of time spent preparing them for sale and then selling them at the door. I think that by the time we've deducted all that, you're going to me owing me money!"

Bob howled in protest while the rest of us fell about laughing. Dad eventually gave him some cash, but I don't think it was as much as Bob had hoped for.

Chapter Fifteen
Bringing Up Father

As you'll have gathered from some of the anecdotes elsewhere in this book, Dad was a character. I've tried to fit stories about him into context with other happenings but inevitably, there are quite a few stories that don't have a 'home,' so they are collected in this chapter.

Dad and Mum celebrating

Looking at old photos, he was thin as a lath until he was about forty and then he started to put on weight and was over twenty stone when he died. It was a source of some amusement to the staff at Rolls Royce at Crewe when they had to specially alter the position of the seat in his car so that he could get his ample girth behind the wheel. Before that was done, Mum suggested that he wear a leather apron when he was out in the car so that the steering wheel wouldn't rub holes in his waistcoat. Dad sniffily declined the suggestion.

Early memories of him included the bedtime stories that he told us of his exploits in Africa with his brothers. Neither he nor his brothers had ever been to Africa, but that didn't limit his imagination. There were always crocodiles and hippopotamuses causing trouble as they travelled about on 'the great, green, greasy Limpopo River, dotted about with fever trees' 'Fever Trees' was always pronounced Fee-ee-eever Tree-ees to emphasise the shaking caused by African fevers.

Dad was very good natured and the only time I heard him lose his temper was when he was being harassed by the Tory bigwigs during the New Market affair. He would often burst into song and waltz around the kitchen with bits remembered from the Music Halls and one favourite was:

"Oh, I went to market with my Uncle Jim

And somebody threw a tomato at him!

Now tomatoes are soft, and they don't hurt the skin

This beggar did, it was still in the tin!"

He had a set of false teeth for his lower jaw and a favourite trick of his to amuse the children and grandchildren was to lift these lower teeth up with his tongue and push them forward so that they stuck out in front of his face. Just like the Gruffalo but without the big tusks. Then he'd make gnashing noises as if he was a fierce monster to shrieks of delight. We were with him once in the new Rolls in Manchester one evening and I think we were coming home from the theatre. We got stopped at some traffic lights and a group of people crossed the road right in front of the car, but one nosy woman broke away from the group and peered in the driver's window presumably to see it was someone famous driving around in a new model Rolls. Dad looked back at her for a second then did his famous 'gnashing' bit at her. She shrieked and ran off while we roared with laughter.

When Linda got engaged her fiancé Peter, he was living on the far side of Manchester at Failsworth. He didn't have a car but came to visit her on his power assisted bicycle. This had a little petrol engine fixed to a frame above the back wheel and it drove the back wheel via a ridged drum that was pressed down firmly onto the rear tyre. If you've seen a VeloSoleX in France, this was just the same sort of thing except that the motor on a VeloSoleX is on the front wheel. It had two simple controls on the handlebars these being a throttle and a little lever that opened a valve in the cylinder head and so stopped the engine firing because there was no longer any compression in the cylinder. So, whenever Peter drove into the yard, he pulled the little lever to prevent compression and then coasted to a halt. The motor was no longer firing but it was still being turned over by the back wheel and so Peter coasted to a stop to a very distinctive *Chuff-a-Chuff-a-Chuff-a-Chuff-a* sound. Of course, it was christened 'The Chuffer'. When Peter and Linda got married, they got to the bit in the wedding service where Peter said:

"And with all my worldly goods I thee endow"

And very distinctly in the hushed church Dad was heard to say, "There goes his Chuffer!"

For some reason, Dad decided at one point to start wearing a monocle. He went to Munich for a European conference on abattoirs, I think he was national chairman for the councils at the time and of course he had to wear his monocle. Inevitably, I suppose, being in Bavaria he was always addressed as Herr Graf which he lapped up but to add to the confusion, when a group of them were in the lift after dinner and all were saying, guten nacht, bon soir and so on, he said "nos da" which is Welsh and caused much head scratching.

Another of Dad's interests was the local Agricultural Society – the Didsbury and South Manchester Agricultural Society. The existence of the Society was based around providing an Annual Show in some playing fields in Didsbury. Dad eventually became Chairman of the Society and so the family got roped in helping to organise the annual Didsbury Show. The society didn't have much in the way of physical assets as just about everything from marquees to seating was hired in. They did own a full set of jumps for show jumping events and these finished up being stored at either Park Brow or Hough End and being fettled up and painted by family and farm hands every year.

The other things they owned included a set of large display boards to which posters were fixed advertising the next Show. These were to be fixed in pre-agreed locations around south Manchester weeks before the next show and many of them went into the entrance to pub car parks. Oliver and I would help out with the poster sticking then go out with Bob to help fix them in their chosen locations. Bob went early one year to the George and Dragon in Cheadle and banged on the door to the pub. An upstairs window opened, and a slatternly woman leaned out shouting:

"Whatcher want?"

Quick as a flash, Bob responded with

"Is George in?"

Fortunately, she didn't get the quip or that would have been the last time we'd have allowed to put a poster there.

The Didsbury Show was always a bit of a family affair and there are photos of Mum looking very smart handing out cups and rosettes. There's also a superb photo of my cousin Margaret who was a very good horsewoman flying over a jump on her horse Crackerjack. We think this photo came from the Manchester Evening News photographer who also snapped me and my brother Oliver driving round the ring in a little cart being pulled by a Shetland pony. I think I'm about four so Oliver would be three and he had lovely blond curls. You look at the photo and you can almost hear the crowd round the ring going "Awwww."

That "Awww…" moment at Didsbury Show 1946

***My cousin Margaret flying over a jump at Didsbury Show on
Crackerjack
You can see how popular the show was from the crowds
around the ring***

The whole family got involved in the Show helping out at everything. One year, Bob was given the job of managing the Collecting Ring which was a small ring next to the Main Ring where riders and horses would wait for their turn in the Main Ring and would also use it to cool off their horses after they'd performed. A very haughty, horsey lady emerged from a show jumping round on a horse that was lathered in sweat from its efforts.

Bob said: "My word! He's sweating a bit!"

"The horsey lady looked down at him and said "Young man. If you'd been between my thighs for the last half hour, you'd be sweating too!"

Didsbury Show was always heavily dependent on the weather being good or else they wouldn't take enough money on the gate to cover their expenses. They were few opportunities for pre-Show ticket sales unlike today's Internet age, so two or three bad weather years could seriously hurt the Society's finances and that's exactly what happened. It was very sad when the Society and its show were wound up because it was a lovely friendly little show.

Many years later, Dad and Mum decided to go to Buenos Aires where Oliver was then working and living with his wife Alicia. It was just after their first daughter Sam was born so a visit to see the new grand-daughter was in order. The house that Oliver and Alicia were renting wasn't that far from the official residence of the President and of course, there were soldiers at every corner. So, when he went for a walk Dad in his monocle would walk past and incline his head and the trooper would spring to attention and salute thinking he was a retired General! Meanwhile Mum was going "Leonard!" each time he did it. There was a sort of zoo, nothing too extensive and as he wanted to see it, he got in a taxi, asking for the zoo and when the taxi driver didn't understand, Dad went "tigre, grr, grr," he got there and back again as Alicia had written down our address. He didn't know how lucky he'd been or perhaps he'd made a very good tiger imitation because slap bang in the opposite direction was a suburb of Buenos Aires, called Tigre.

Another feat of his down there was the Mate. Mate is a South American beverage that is a sort of green tea that is drawn up through a straw from a small gourd also called a Mate and after being refilled with hot water, it's passed to the next person to partake. He expressed surprise at Alicia's parents doing this, filling, passing along so many times and at the local ironmongers somehow managed to buy a small clay pot that would hold about a litre, copper tubing to make the six straws, complete with mesh filters and not forgetting the paint to adorn it. This was presented to Alicia's parents to their great delight and Oliver was doubled up laughing when Dad explained that it had to be easier for all of them to drink at the same time. It was proudly on display in their house for years and years.

They unwittingly had a very narrow escape from death when leaving Argentina for home in May 1972. They were booked to sail home on the *Royston Grange*, a refrigerated Cargo liner that carried frozen products as well as a dozen passengers. They decided to stay a few more days and re-booked their passage home on another ship, thus saving their lives. In the early hours of May 11, the *Royston Grange* was in collision in fog with a tanker carrying crude oil on the River

Plate. The tanker immediately set on fire and explosions carried the fire across to the ***Royston Grange*** which burned particularly hot as she was carrying butter and oil. All the sixty-one crew and twelve passengers on the ***Royston Grange*** were killed. There is an article about the fate of the Royston Grange on Wikipedia, and it is a sobering read.

I've mentioned that Dad liked his fishing and he had a good selection of rods and reels for both sea and river fishing. Armed with these, he'd go on a week's fishing holiday every year with Uncle Will and Uncle Seymour. They usually went to the West coast of Ireland fishing in Loch Corrib not far from Galway and sometimes a bit further north in Loch Conn. They used to get the ferry from Holyhead to Dublin and then get across Ireland by train. They'd come back with presents for us all and stories of what they'd been up to. The journey across Ireland usually involved at least one change of train and they told us that they often had long waits for their connections due to the vagaries of the Irish Rail System – lack of coal, lack of water, lack of drivers/firemen, cattle on the line.... They just had to learn to be patient. At one little country station in later years, my uncles decided to pass a few minutes by weighing themselves on the scales on the platform. They then put a penny in the slot and badgered Dad, who was by now pretty heavy, to get on so that they could find out what he really weighed. Dad stepped on and the needle whipped round, hit the stop and promptly bent! They'd neglected to tell him that the scales only went up to 14 stone! What the station staff said when they found it would be good to know.

The three of them regularly used to argue with each other using the well-worn standard Bailey method of reasoned discussion. Flat statement, followed by flat contradiction, followed by personal abuse. Unwary fellow train passengers would sometimes intervene, on one occasion it was a priest, to find that all three brothers had now shifted their perspective and they were now teamed up against the interloper. They were known as "The Brothers that Argue"

One of their most famous arguments was over the lineage of a champion Shire horse mare named Erfyl Lady Grey. All three of them were of a farming generation that used heavy horses, so they were all proud of their knowledge of which were the best and where to go to buy a good one. On this occasion, they were all staying at Uncle Will's farm at Cors-y-Gedol and the row broke out late in the evening when they were all in the library. Each of the three had a different opinion about which horse was the mare that had given birth to Erfyl Lady Grey, the champion Shire horse. The row got louder and more heated and those not involved retreated to the kitchen. From there, they eventually heard:

"I'm not listening to any more of this rubbish. I'm off to bed!" *SLAM* as the library door was forcibly shut.

Shortly afterwards, it was:

"And I'm telling you you're bloody wrong!" *SLAM*

There the matter simmered for a few days, but Dad wasn't one to give up easily and managed to find a book of Shire horse lineage which covered the two horses in question. And he was right! He chuckled hugely and said "Wait 'til those two buggers are next here and then I'll show 'em!"

A few weeks went by and both Uncle Will and Uncle Seymour came round and after lunch, Dad casually said:

"You know that discussion we were having on Shire horses a few weeks ago? Well I've found a Stud Book that's got the answer in it." And he smiled, knowing that it would prove him right.

He put the book on the table and all three looked down at it. Uncle Will read it and shut it and then said just two words that summed up their debating skills perfectly:

"Book's wrong!"

Chapter Sixteen
Uncle Will and The Welsh Connection

My Uncle Will was the oldest of my uncles and had fought in the First World War. He was in the Machine Gun Corps and later the 51st Highland Division and had fought and survived the horrors of the Somme. He also famously remarked after his time with the Highlanders that he found the Scots more trouble than the Germans! He married my Aunt Hannah and set up in a farm not far from Stockport in Cheshire at Underbank Farm and later at a place called Bradshaw Hall Farm. After he left Bradshaw Hall, the whole estate was acquired by Stockport UDC who demolished the old hall and the farm and then cleared the whole area so that it is now a large housing estate.

Uncle Will and his family then moved to North Wales where they acquired Cors-y-Gedol Hall and its farming estate just a few miles north of Barmouth. The Hall dates from the 16th century and is an impressive stone-built affair with an imposing Gate House standing just in front of the main entrance. The Gate House is notable for being built with an arch through the middle of it so that carriages could pass through it and it also has a very old clock in its central clock tower that has only a single hand showing the hours, so you have to estimate the minutes. To one side of the hall was the Home Farm and Will's eldest son Eddie lived there with his wife Janet and there was a maze of farm buildings close by. There was even a rather nice ornamental lake beside the house in which we tried our hand at fishing using long bamboos that we'd cut from a clump that was growing handily beside the lake.

The front of Cors y Gedol Hall and the Gatehouse

The main business of the farm was sheep and they had thousands of them. The estate was apparently of about 3000 acres and within its boundaries were a mountain (Moelfre) and three lakes one of which, Lyn Bodlyn, was a reservoir supplying water to Barmouth. The shepherds who took care of the sheep had so much ground to cover that they couldn't cover the ground on foot and had to use ex-army jeeps. When the sheep had to be brought down from the hills it was a major operation to round them up for dipping and shearing so vehicles packed with men and dogs disappeared in all directions before returning late in the day, slowly driving the sheep in front of them.

Once Uncle Will and his family had settled in, the rest of his brothers wanted to see what he was up to and so went down to visit him. We went as a family in the big old Rolls and turned north from Barmouth onto the coast road leading to Harlech. We turned off the main road onto a driveway that was flanked by two attractive little gate house cottages then set off up the drive. And what a drive. It was a mile long and straight as an arrow until you turned off at the top when you saw the unique Gatehouse with its one-handed clock. The hall itself could only just be made out behind the gatehouse and looked a bit grim as it was built of grey stone and had rather small mullioned windows. It looked really old and made quite an impression on a nine-year-old. You could imagine centuries of adventures having taken place there.

The hall had plenty of rooms so putting family up wasn't a problem, but I seem to remember that we took our own bedding. When we first went, we got the tour and were suitably impressed by the baronial splendour of the Big Hall with its massive fireplace and the beautifully panelled dining room off it. On a cosier scale was the library and a large drawing room which had been decorated in the style of Robert Adam. Other large rooms set further back included one with a full-size snooker table in it that was very popular with us boys and a ballroom. Ballrooms are not a lot of use on working farms so on our first visit, the ballroom was being used to house orphaned lambs with straw bales and assorted dividers set up to provide corrals for the lambs. Oliver and I got to bottle feed them on the few mornings of our stay.

When we left the Hall and farm buildings for a walk with Uncle Will, we set off uphill on a stony track towards the hills, heading for the area where the sheep were to be penned and dipped. The track ran alongside a stream and Uncle Will said:

"Can you see something funny about the stream?"

We looked around and didn't see what we were supposed to see so he gave us a hint.

"Well, are we going uphill or downhill?" and we said that at this point we were definitely going downhill.

"So, what's the stream doing alongside us?" and we twigged. The stream was coming towards us heading towards to the sea but the path we were on was definitely sloping downwards away from the sea. The stream was flowing uphill! It was obviously an optical illusion, but it was very convincing then, and it still is.

Alongside the path was a small stone-built building from which could be heard the faint whine of machinery.

"What's that?" we said.

"That's the turbine house. It's where we generate all the electricity for the hall and farm"

Uncle Will explained that there was a pipe let into the bed of the stream quite a distance up hill and it led direct to the turbine house. By the time it reached there, the water had dropped a couple of hundred feet or so and thus came out with terrific force to drive the turbine which was coupled to a generator. They had virtually free electricity despite having no mains supply. There were however a couple of snags. The first and most important was that the generator, which had been installed many years before the war, only supplied 110 volts so any electrical equipment had to suit this. Toasters, irons, fridges and even light bulbs had to be 110 volt. Their main source was the Yanks. In the 1950s, there were American bases all over Britain and they were using imported American domestic appliances all at 110 volts. So, Uncle Will and Eddie made contact with US bases and managed to source most of what they needed.

The other snag with the system was poachers. Uncle Will's family would be sitting round the fire in the evening when the lights would start to go dim.

"Poachers!" went up the cry and any men folk would grab shotguns, jump into a jeep and set off up the track to the lake. The poachers would of course hear the jeep and see its lights, so they always scarpered before anyone arrived. Then it was a job to walk beside the stream with big torches looking for the temporary dam that the poachers had put in to help them catch fish but whose side effect had been to stop the flow of water to the turbine. I'm sure the poachers must have wondered how their activity was caught on to so quickly.

The Hall had been originally built in the 16th century by the Vaughan family and altered and extended by the family over the next 200 years. It is understood that was an earlier Hall on the site, also built by the Vaughans and there was a novel appropriately called '*The Lord of Cors y Gedol*' about the family. In the novel, the Lord named Rhys Vaughan, imprisons one of his daughters, referred to the book as 'The Fair Agnes', in an attic room to prevent her running off with a shepherd boy that the Lord disapproves of. The imprisoned daughter wrote messages to her lover on strips of material torn from her clothes using her own blood as ink. The messages were exchanged between the lovers by means of dove which would fly into the attic room through an open window.

Uncle Will told us, with great relish, that the ghosts of the lovers still haunted the place and that he could prove it because there was one attic room with a broken pane of glass in the window and whenever he replaced it, it was always broken within a week, so that a ghostly dove could fly in. He showed us the room with its broken window and from then on, we kept well away from that part of the house. There was an amusing sequel to this tale when Ronnie Rushton who was courting Uncle Will's younger daughter Margaret, came to stay at the Hall. Needless to say, that first evening he was filled up with stories about the history of the Hall including the one about the ghost of Fair Agnes told at great length. He was sleeping that night in what was known as the Queen's Bedroom when something woke him up and as he looked up, he saw something white and wraith-like drift past the windows. He yelled out and every one of the few hairs that he had on his head stood on end. Next morning Uncle Will roared with laughter when he was told the tale of the apparition. "That was no ghost" he guffawed. "It was the barn owl that roosts in the tree outside your window!"

He liked to tell stories and one night he spoke a little about things that happened to him in France in the First World War. He told how once he had been on lookout when he saw a cloud coming towards their trenches and realised that it was poison gas. They had dugouts well below the trenches, so he quickly grabbed the lintel to one of the stairways leading down to the dugout and swung himself down the stairs. He skidded off the top step and bumped on his backside down the steps for about 30 feet and was so sore that he couldn't sit down for a week. He grabbed for his gas mask but couldn't put it on straight away as it was made of leather and the leather was dry and not flexible enough to fit tightly to his face. He said that he had to pee on the gas mask and work it into the leather to make it supple enough to work!

Another of his tales concerned his wife Hannah and he told us this after her death. According to Uncle Will, she had some gipsy blood in her ancestry and could tell fortunes and summon up spirits. He said that she could read tea leaves and palms and she was very accurate at both. He also said that he kept well out of the way when she gathered round like-minded friends to work a Ouija board and to do table tapping. He said that he once looked out of the room in time to see Hannah and three friends with their hands resting lightly on the top of a large oak dining table and the table was several inches off the floor and moving slowly down the hall with the four women around it.

Was it true? I guess we'll never know. He may have just been making it up to give us a scare. If so, he succeeded.

Uncle Will as the oldest of the five brothers was the nominal head of the family. When I got engaged, Uncle Will was summoned from Wales as head of the family to meet my wife-to-be, Vicky, more as a courtesy than to see if she was suitable. He looked at her and said. "She'll do fine. She's a bonny little thing and she's got good child-bearing hips!" There's a farmer's judgement for you!

His grandsons and great grandsons are still at Cors y Gedol though the hall isn't lived in but is now used as a wedding venue. I hope that Fair Agnes and her ghostly dove don't trouble the newlyweds.

Chapter Seventeen
Oliver's Travels

My younger brother Oliver went on to have a rather adventurous life travelling around the world building power lines and pylons. As he was very much a part of my young life and this is a family story, it seemed right to invite him to add a chunk to this book about what befell him in Northern Ireland, Iran and South America so this chapter is very much in his own words:

"Sit down lad and I'll you a tale of foreign parts, places that even Heineken might not have reached. Only the faithful native bearers driving Land Rovers and a few tormented souls who ventured far and wide to build electricity pylons to bring power to mad scientists everywhere, and even a few sane ones I suppose.

It all started with a case of mistaken identity; I wrote to one company to apply for a job and to my surprise I was being interviewed by another company, a part of the main group, but they built things rather than making them and the things they built were electricity pylons, all over the world. I was young, I was unattached, and I was mad, so they signed me up, poor fools.

A short induction course on the basics, and it was only two weeks, then I was sent to Northumberland. In Winter. But at least I got free wellies, and I needed them. It was probably the last of the cowboy trades; you would pitch up in some unsuspecting locality, find a place to stay, usually a pub, a place to have an office and store and over time several dozen hard drinking people would arrive. In the early sixties redundant railway stations were popular as there were station buildings and hard ground to lay out our stuff and if any of the *people had a caravan, there were connections for utilities and parking space for all the strange equipment we used, most of it unique to the overhead line industry.*

All that is background to the community of people in the business and a large number of them were larger than life characters, the stuff of industry legend. Two I knew were accomplished poachers and one of them, having taken four salmon from the Coquet was on his way home one night when he was stopped by the police looking for turkey thieves. Tommy thought his number was up but when the law realised, he had only salmon, they were very understanding and let him go. Turkey stealing was taking away a man's livelihood, but salmon weren't anyone's property, except perhaps in the eyes of some rich chap who owned a stretch of riverbank the fish happened to be passing. Anyway, salmon steaks were always welcomed by the Sergeant.

The other one I knew worked in Northern Ireland and Jimmy could feed his large family on what he took out of Lough Erne. He used otter boards, gelignite, seine nets, whatever worked, but his main use to us was that he was superb at repairing the dry-stone walls we happened to damage and there were a lot of those in Ulster. It seems almost inconceivable now but one day I turned up at the main explosives store in Northern Ireland, presented my letter of authorisation and I drove away, on my own, with fifty pounds of dynamite and two boxes of electric detonators. As I had to keep the latter away from the former, the explosives were in the boot and detonators on the passenger seat. In the films, it all looks very technical and dramatic with twisting keys and pushing down on plungers, but we just picked up the two wires and touched the terminals on a convenient battery, usually that of an air compressor; just as effective and less likely to go wrong. Health and Safety existed, but in those days, they were hitting the big numbers in factories and so on; out in the wilds it was a different story. Every person had to wear a safety helmet but the designs available in those days were useless if you were high in the air because they were more likely to fall off in the wind and hit someone on the ground. Safety belts too. All climbers had to have a safety belt but the law as it was didn't require them to attach them to anything so mostly, they stayed in the vehicle. However

136

standing instructions were that if someone fell off a tower, you fitted a safety belt and then checked for injuries. Or just leave one lying nearby and say you had taken it off when the ambulance came.

Down in excavations safety helmets were needed but getting people to wear them was an ongoing battle and sadly, I was less than two months into my career when a guy was killed by a falling rock when he was at the bottom of the excavation. What affected everyone on site was that even if he had been wearing a hard hat, it wouldn't have saved him because he was kneeling down, and the rock hit him on the back of the neck and broke it. Ironically, his job as a timber man was to fit the supports to the sides of the hole so others could work in relative safety. This provoked a lot of soul searching on how to do things better and one lunchtime in our local, the Railway Inn in Rothbury and, believe it or not, on the back of a fag packet, I sketched out an expanding hydraulic support frame that could be lowered down and positioned from above, so there would be basic support to the sides in place before anybody went down to fix the more permanent framework.

I was an apprentice at the time, so I didn't acquire any rights over my invention, but the company did build some and I was told later that one had proved to be an astonishing success because the sides started to collapse just after the frame had been positioned. Maybe I should have left and gone into business, but I reckoned that first I would have had to buy the rights to my own invention.

I did spend an interesting two weeks just over the Scottish border in Lauder where the landlady was a cordon bleu chef and bred champion dachshunds. The three of us fed like fighting cocks, washed up behind the bar and even cashed up at night. That was the only occasion I ever saw a policeman kicked out of a pub as we were drinking late with local worthies and the Provost of Lauder took umbrage at his audacity, "Get out man, these gentlemen are drinking with the Provost of Lauder." Said constable knew he had to live in the town and left. Later the same night, a local farmer, Tom was too drunk to drive so I was recruited by the Provost to follow in his car while he drove Tom home. Tom was propped against the door and when his wife saw the state he was in she started to berate

137

him until she saw the Provost and invited the two of us in. She brought out the Crawford's Five Star whisky for us and when Tom asked for some, his lady told him in no uncertain terms that his chances were nil and two drams later we left, and the Provost dropped me back at the Black Bull.

Two evenings later, when we were washing up the glasses, Gordon asked what had happened to the automatic glass washer that was set into the bar top. Jean's response was "you are engineers, you fix it." a challenge we had to accept, without a manual, without tools and without the faintest idea what happened even when it was in working order. By the process of elimination, we deduced the fault lay in a faulty pressure switch and on taking it apart, discovered the rubber diaphragm had perished. Les borrowed a pair of scissors and cut a circle out of a plastic bottle and lo and behold, it worked. Lights came on, the conveyor started running and hot water sprayed over the glasses as they were moved along on the rubber belts. The main problem was it was too slow to cope with an active crowd of drinkers, but we did get a free drink for our pains.

Four months later I was given my own contract to run, dismantling a redundant power line just outside Stockton. It had its ups and downs and the downs were the bit I enjoyed. Most of the gang would be working ahead removing the cables and insulators etc while I was with one guy and a Land Rover. He would attach a rope to the top while I used the acetylene torch on the legs and then as we drove away, down came the tower. In fact, we became so good that we could put a stick in the ground marking where the tower would fall with a satisfying thump.

After the frozen North-East, it was over the Irish Sea to Ulster. Northern Ireland in the late sixties was a good place to be, drink and drive laws were a foreign oddity, which was perhaps as well given the amount of Bushmills whisky we downed. However, there was a single drawback, pubs were closed on Sundays. Apart from the clubs. And thanks to friends in the Northern Ireland orchestra I was made welcome in the BBC club, known to it habitués as the English Embassy.

Within our somewhat closed group, there wasn't even a hint of religious conflict. We had both left and right footers in the same gang and on the Feasts of Obligation, the Catholics would take time out to attend Mass and then pitch in by working late. As an Englishman I wasn't seen as involved with either side and in the same week I was invited to march with the Orange Order and judge a beauty competition sponsored by a Catholic Church. Guess which won?

I rounded up two friends and we arrived about eight in the evening to this small town and knocked on the door of the priest's house. I introduced myself and we three were sent to the local pub, closed on a Sunday of course, but the priest's helper knocked on the door, the Judas hatch opened, and the landlord was told we had been sent by the Father. Door opens, Black Bushmills provided, and we settled down to wait the call. As a beauty contest it wasn't going to put Miss World out of business, it was just the local girls and was part of a dance night with the added challenge that the three judges had to select the girls to take part. I had been invited as a complete outsider, apparently there had been skulduggery in the past and there was I, a lapsed Anglican, at a dance in a Catholic church asking complete strangers to take part in a beauty contest. Some turned me down, as the habits of swinging London in the 1960s hadn't reached that corner of the Six Counties and the young ladies were more reserved. However, one I picked out won that night and went on to the regional finals.

I was next off to Iran, which was interesting, perhaps even in the sense of "may you live in interesting times", but the Shah was still on the Peacock Throne, this was ten years before his overthrow, but even I, a farangi, could tell he wasn't that popular. However, we had a job to do and that was to construct *over five hundred kilometres of power line from a hydro dam, MRSP, in the south, through the Zagros Mountains to Tehran via a place called Arak, of which more later. This had its complications. One of which was that in Iran there was no compulsory insurance for vehicles, so if someone got killed in a road accident, the driver stayed in jail until the blood price was agreed. Regrettably of the four ex-pats in the office three were involved in fatal accidents, though one was a suicide we learnt later, as was our local fixer, a very capable Armenian gent. If you were in jail, the food was as good as your friends brought you and visiting was fairly relaxed until one day, I went to see one guy and the Police Chief, a very jovial fellow addressed me with a laugh, saying he was looking forward to having me as an official guest because I was the only one he hadn't locked up. Still, we got on well and one day he sent over some caviar that (gasp, shock, horror) two of us consumed with baked beans, as to us they were the real luxury. I'll bet Heston Blumenthal hasn't tried that one.*

We had to build our own roads through the mountains and in spring and autumn the Bakhtiari nomads extensively used them as they walked to and from upland pastures. Very friendly people but it was difficult even with an interpreter at hand because of their dialect. A few of us got invited to their camp one night and we ate goat and rice washed down with vodka and 7 Up and they taught us to dance Bakhtiari style – men only of course. Some of us got invited to weddings in the Armenian community, with a half bottle of vodka each as a place setting and we were allowed to dance with the young ladies, but only if there was a visible space between us at all times.

In the winter it snows, and it snows, and it snows, and wolves could be a problem. We always thought that the Weather Forecast should include the useful information of "Light to moderate descents of wolves are expected in ......" We had to close most of the camps and we mostly headed down to the southernmost one, near the hydro dam at a place called Andimeshk. It was all very convivial but crowded though one of the blessings was that the cook could prepare superb apple pies, of which there was never enough. Knowing that one of our brethren, Mike, had a delicate constitution, once the apple pie was on the table, Harry and myself would start to discuss the terrible road accidents we had seen, all imaginary of course, but with enough gory details, Mike would flee the mess heaping curses on our heads.

As is almost inevitable in the rush for progress in one section, there were errors in installing the foundations and it fell to me to demolish them and reinstall in the right place – I am talking errors of centimetres here but with prefabricated steel there was little tolerance. Bringing to the fore my limited experience of blowing things up in Northern Ireland, we managed to get reasonably efficient then one day I was summoned to a meeting at the main construction office. There, a man from the Ministry of Water and Power, together with the number two from the consulting engineers informed me that we had been denounced to the secret police –SAVAK – because we had installed duff concrete. The mention of SAVAK was enough to get those two gents in a flap as they are seriously unpleasant people and guess who was volunteered to sort it all out.

All I knew was that he had a little list and it was down to me to prove our concrete was sound at the locations that we wouldn't know about until the day. Some sleight of hand was needed, and I had a piece of kit called a Schmitt Hammer that gives an indication of the concrete strength by measuring the impact resistance. Armed with this, and not a little apprehension, we awaited the arrival of the Colonel. Said Colonel turned up in a huge Chrysler Monaco and could have stood in for the baddie in many films without even changing his dark glasses and I was given the number of the first tower position he wanted to check. I guided them there and I explained to the Colonel how the gubbins worked, even handing over the chart so he could compare the readings on the Schmitt with the strength it represented. First one a resounding success, then another and then another until after we had done five or six the Colonel, demanded to see where we were working. As I already knew he would be making a "surprise" visit, things were as perfect as they could be and said Colonel was heaping imprecations on the snitch, leaving in a huff. The thing is that with a Schmitt Hammer in the hands of an unscrupulous person, the readings can be enhanced sufficiently to avoid anyone spending time as a guest in Evin Prison.

Ministry guy heaped blessings on my head and I retired to drink a well-earned vodka or two.

One of our site stores was in a place called Khorramabad, a place of ill-repute, renowned for the light-fingered populace who would steal anything that they were capable of carrying away, so the camp employed a significant number of watchmen during the day and more than twice as many at night. Local etiquette required that the local headman was asked to provide watchmen and after picking his relatives and adding others who would pay a kickback, he provided the required number of warm bodies, whom we paid as part of the cost of doing business there. In the course of time as activities flowed and ebbed, we reduced the number of watchmen required and one sued us for unfair dismissal. As the ex-pat in charge of the camp was a little casual in such matters it was not unexpected but what emerged at the hearing was that said night watchman was blind and had been from birth.

Barely suppressed chortles on the British side, how can there be a sustainable case for a blind watchman? However, the judge was absolutely correct and fair in his decision; the man had been blind from birth, so that fact hadn't been an impediment to him being hired, perhaps we had wanted him for his acute hearing? So, the case had to be decided on the merits in law, not on his physical condition and we lost. Richard Dawkins might have envisaged a blind watchmaker, but we had had a real blind watchman.

I mentioned Arak earlier and this became my base as it was about in the middle of the line and there was to be a largish sub-station to feed local demand and later, this was expanded to receive power from another dam, RSK. While it might not have been in the Shah's mind in the 1960s, Arak was where Iran later developed its nuclear engineering capability, but it was a great place to live and work at the time. As a coda to my time there, in the early eighties, after the revolution, our valuation and claims manager was on a visit to tidy up the last project and he came across an engineer who remembered me. This wasn't the nice guy whose head I had saved, it was one who had been fairly junior in the 1960s but had risen, probably through revolutionary fervour, and apparently, he had hinted, not that subtly, that my name was on a list of people for whom a dark alley was waiting. Whether or not he was winding Dave up I will never know, and I have never wanted to find out.

Returning after a year, I had declined an offer to renew my contract, I was posted to Brighouse where we were building another line that passed through Bronte country. All very picturesque when the weather was good, but the heights of the Pennines were very wuthering when it rained and blew. And it did. A lot. I got on well with the contract manager and one day Jimmy said there were two tasks that day and he was doing the one that didn't involve the press, so there was I in the middle of a muddy field trying to wax lyrical about my work and as there was a lot of low cloud, the pylons seemed quite ghostly in the mist. Anyway, there were no calls for my head on a platter from the client and I believe Dad tracked down the newspaper article. Great lad our Jimmy; he had just come from the filling station where he had met a lady in distress as she was locked out of her car and he had told her that he'd send me over to open it for her. Were breaking and entering skills in my personnel record as well? Anyway, in those days two thin strips of metal and knight errantry had done its bit. The lady, though grateful, was somewhat horrified at how easy it had been.

When I saw a call for someone to go to Argentina, I hastened to put down my name, it sounded a lot better than Brighouse in winter. I passed being interviewed by personnel, the project manager and the general manager so there I was at Gatwick, dressed in a hastily bought lightweight suit to be able to greet Buenos Aires in midsummer, being told that I was to be routed via Zurich, the next day. Jetways were for the future at the time, so transfers were done by bus and it was well below zero at Kloten as I disembarked and later re-embarked for the long flight south. The problem was all this had happened late at night, so I was hoping that somehow, whoever was going to meet the earlier flight would be there a day later. Janusz Wroblewicz was and he became one of my best friends, he even introduced me to the lady who became my wife.

Dealing with any Government is a pain, but under Juan Peron we suffered, or rather the transmission line did, assault by tornados, which brought down seven towers and blacked out Buenos Aires. They were not amused. Our design used stays to hold the things up, common elsewhere in the world, but a first

143

in *Argentina, and President Peron denounced us on national television as having tied them up with baling wire. This was a bit of a comedown from a year previously when all the companies involved in the massive project had been praised for bringing the project in right on the nose, another first for Argentina (and deeply resented by their establishment). There again, the inauguration of the project had been carried out with a sense of the absurd, because a dam had been built, turbines and generators installed, a thousand kilometres of transmission line constructed and all they could was open the spillway and let water out of the lake. Why? Because the state electricity company hadn't built the 30km of line to connect it to the city; they had procrastinated as ever because they couldn't believe the project would come in on time.*

Of course, there was great tumult and shouting and, in the end, we had to agree to reinforce the foundations on about half the line and I was selected from a pool of one to carry it out, without turning off the electricity! But our woes didn't end there. Argentina is vast and in the direction we went, flat, and I mean flat because in a thousand kilometres the ground rose less than 300 m and as such is a breeding ground for tornadoes, and we were the weather gauge.

Nobody had cottoned on to this beforehand; the loss of the odd barn or stand of trees was hardly worthy of comment and now we were being hit with F4 tornadoes, very strong winds indeed. And they came back again and again. About three times a year our intrepid band, a foreman and me as the only expats, rallied the ranks and put the perishing things up again. Thanks to Andy we became quite expert and in the five years from the first collapse we replaced about fifty; an expensive weather gauge but representing as it did about one percent of the total, in military terms, acceptable losses.

There was also the entertaining business of the gaucho Carruthers. For those who do not know, an Argentine gaucho (cowboy) has a very distinctive form of dress and as we worked our way across the desert part of Argentina, we had set up camps for the work force and they were still in use as a base for maintenance even after the construction was finished. Three of us were journeying back by road from the El Chocon dam in the foothills of the Andes looking in at the camps to determine their future and that evening we stopped at the one in Lihue Calel. Knowing who'd be there, Dave and myself kept shtum and sent Tom on ahead to knock on the door and see if the watchman had arrived. When the door was opened by someone in full gaucho regalia, Tom tried to greet him in halting Spanish. To our mirth, poor Tom was totally taken aback to be greeted by this gaucho in perfect Home Counties English, "Good evening, won't you come in, I am just listening to the BBC World Service." The little we knew of his background was that Carruthers was the black sheep of the family, sent abroad a few decades previously for blotting the family escutcheon and had adopted the life of a gaucho, but instead of a horse, he drove a Model A Ford to work.

Even in the flat country there were sights of extraordinary beauty, and one that stays with me is setting off very early one morning and disturbing the wild life at a lake and I saw the incredible sight of a flock of flamingos rising up with dawn's light illuminating their pink plumage.

Living out in the countryside had its compensations. Half a dozen of us were out checking the transmission line and we stopped for lunch at cantina. We had barbecued beef, salad, wine and coffee all for the extortionate price of £1.50. For the six of us! Some of these were guys I knew in Northumberland I met again in Argentina and Colombia then later in Hong Kong and South Africa. Some were very exotic characters. Alfred was one who had fled Poland and once in Britain, joined the SOE getting parachuted into Yugoslavia using the nom de guerre of Captain Link becoming great friends with Tito and Fitzroy MacLean. Also, I believe, Randolph Churchill. In addition, in his youth he had become friends with the guy who became John Paul II and when he was on the rails with the crowd greeting him when he was the Pope, he got recognised by the Pontiff who refused to let him kneel. His marriage certificate was unusual because in the place where you put occupation of bride's father, it was written, "Russian General". He was an ace fixer of damn nearly anything in the local bureaucracy for us. A strange fraternity; we few, we happy few, we band of brothers.

Contrary to what you might think, Buenos Aires can be damn cold in winter and I had bought my wife Alicia a mink coat, so of course she took it with her when we went to London one February. I had to spend a fair bit of time in head office, so she had gone shopping and we had arranged to meet in the lobby before we went back to the hotel. My boss had wanted to meet her, so we stayed for a while chatting and as we were leaving who should come in but the Executive Director with his wife. We were introduced, and it was pretty obvious that said lady was very miffed that my wife had a mink coat and she didn't! Worse still, Alicia was wearing it with jeans! I have no doubt his ear was severely bent once they were alone. Hardly worthy of comment but the upshot was I had an external auditor come in to the office in Buenos Aires, but he wouldn't say why, and I only found out later he was checking all the bank statements and in particular, my expenses. I still cherish the thought that the Executive Director had spent about three thousand pounds of the company's money to appease his envious wife.

After a stint in Hong Kong I was back in Argentina working with a company that did electrical-mechanical stuff and an offshoot had various agencies, including Rolls Royce gas turbines. Why might that be significant? Well the following tale is absolutely true. Argentina invaded the Falklands on the 2ⁿᵈ April 1982 and a week later I was working late when the telephone rang; on answering it I learnt that the caller was a Rear Admiral in the Argentine Navy and he wanted spare parts for the Olympus gas turbines that powered some of his ships. Mustering all my self-possession I managed to transfer the call to the man who ran the agency side, and only then could I smile at the irony of it. With that kind of forward planning, they were going to lose.

A great friend of mine had flown Hurricanes in the Battle of Britain as a member of one of the Polish squadrons and this was fairly widely known. In those days, to run a business in Argentina it was essential to get on well with the military so, one day after the British Fleet had set sail to liberate the Falklands, he was called to Army HQ. There he was shown a map of the Falklands and asked the question, "You have fought in a war with the British, where do you think they will land?"

Stan pointed out five spots on the map and the planners looked at him in amazement. "But none are near Port Stanley, how will they cross the island?"

Stan's response, "You haven't seen these b***ers march." Of the spots Stan had picked out, the British used three.

At one point in my life I was based in Sao Paulo running two contracts in three different countries using four currencies and working in five separate cities with six project managers trying to build seven submarine cable landing stations, but the best memory is of sitting in a bar in Rio de Janeiro drinking caipirinha and looking out of the window where Tom Jobim had seen and later written about "The Girl from Ipanema."

Approaching sixty and needing employment to keep me occupied and put food on the table, I started work for AWE, the Atomic Weapons Establishment but what can I tell you about my work at Aldermaston? In a word: Nothing. Though from then on, the family always introduced me to their friends as:

"This is Oliver. He's our Weapons of Mass Destruction man!"

Chapter Eighteen

The Sewage Works Has A Lot to Answer For

Once I'd left school, I entered Manchester University to study Biochemistry. I'd no real idea what Biochemistry was about but it seemed to be one of the coming scientific disciplines in the 1950s. Though I was living at home, I did the usual stupid first year student things like drinking far too much and not working very hard. When the summer vacation loomed, I needed something to do rather than just help around the farm and a job appeared in my field as a temporary assistant Analyst at Manchester's Sewage Works at Davyhulme. I went for interview and my face seemed to fit so I started working there very shortly. It was not what I expected as the place was a riot. If you're dealing with s**t on a regular basis, and in large quantities, you need a sense of humour. And that lot had it in spades. It was also where I learned the importance of always washing my hands before eating my sandwiches!

To understand what I was I doing, you first need to know a bit how a sewage works operates. Basically, bacteria digest all the oo-er-nasties and if they're allowed to finish the job, you actually get pure drinking water out at the end of the process. You've probably seen those little sewage works from the train that are circular and have slowly rotating arms on top. All they are doing is sprinkling the effluent (let's call it that from now on, shall we?) onto a bed of charcoal or coke where the bacteria live, and they do the job. This process is fine for small rural communities but for a big city like Manchester you have to scale the job up thousands of times. They used something with the delightful name of the Activated Sludge Process. This uses lots of large ponds to hold the effluent on its way through the process and you then use mechanical means to aerate the liquid to speed up the bacterial digestion process. The aeration can be done in several ways and Manchester had installed three different systems on test before selecting the one they wanted. They had one that was a bit like a river with a serpentine channel that the effluent flowed through and was artificially aerated with a giant stainless-steel brush that beat the surface of the liquid as it flowed through. Another had several rotating steel brushes on a rectangular tank but the best, and the one that Manchester had selected was the Simplex which was a 'slinger'. There was a big (about 40 feet square) concrete tank and in the middle was a large inverted cone powered by an electric motor. The cone had angled blades inside so that when it was powered up, it rotated, and it drew the effluent up and sprayed it across the surface of the tank thus giving it a good old aerating. This was entertaining to watch but you had to be careful that you didn't get sprayed as it certainly hurled the effluent some distance when it was up to speed.

After aerating, the liquid passed through a series of settlement tanks with the liquid getting gradually cleaner and clearer and the exhausted bacteria settling as a sludge. Eventually the cleaned water was emptied into the Manchester Ship Canal while the sludge was scraped up and stored for disposal later. A little-known fact about Manchester was that the City Council were ship owners and '*The Mancunian*' was a ship specially designed to collect the sludge from the holding tanks. Then the ship transported it down the Manchester Ship Canal to dump it at sea beyond the Mersey Bar. Manchester was doing this until 1998 though in reduced quantities because they'd found a way of digesting the sludge to produce Methane and this was used to fuel massive generators that powered most of the plant at Davyhulme.

So how had Manchester decided which aeration system was best? Well that was where the testing laboratory that I was working at came in. When the bacteria, which are naturally occurring, are working away they are using up Oxygen, so samples were taken every day from all round the works and their oxygen consumption was measured. This included dodging the flying effluent in the Simplex tanks. The lower the oxygen demand of the bacteria, the more complete the process is and by the time it reaches the outlet into the Ship Canal (the outfall), it should be zero. We also sampled the water in the Ship Canal above and below the outfall and it was always cleaner below our outfall than above, so there was plenty of gunge in the Ship Canal before it got diluted with our output. Comparisons of the oxygen demand at the start and end of each of the 3 systems under test and related to the throughput had told the researchers which system was best. It was apparently the first time in the world that anyoné had carried out this sort of work and fully developed the Activated Sludge Process.

They were still building the new Works when I arrived and the enormous site of about 120 acres was a maze of massive concrete holding tanks being built with excavators and dump trucks charging along the narrow causeways between them. The laboratory was at the centre of the maze and when arriving by scooter and later car, you had to keep a wary eye out for flying dump trucks. Also, surprisingly there wasn't much of a niff in the air. The lab staff were very friendly and had a robust sense of humour that spilled over into practical jokes. They explained what my job was to be, which was mainly to help in taking the samples, running the tests and recording the results which kept the management informed as to how well the plant was running.

We started off with a guided tour which took quite a long time because the site was so big. I was introduced to some of the key personnel including the redoubtable Arthur Dixon who was the Rivers Inspector. More of him later. They pointed out the various drivers of excavators and dump trucks and in particular to keep well out of the way of the Cisco Kid who took no prisoners and delighted in scaring other site users with the wild driving of his vast dump truck along the narrow causeways. You could usually spot him coming by the large plume of dust that invariably followed his speedy truck and just to reinforce the message, he'd painted CISCO on to top of his cab and he wore an old cowboy hat. I was shown the engine house with its enormous gas/diesel driven generators that could generate three megawatts. This system was just coming on stream though they hadn't finished completing all of the 4 massive digesters that would convert the left-over sludge from the plant into methane to power the generators.

It was all fascinating stuff and I quickly settled in to the routine. We were usually pretty busy in the mornings taking yesterday's samples out of the incubators where they had been overnight and running the tests on them. Then it was off round the site collecting today's samples and getting them started for their overnight run. The afternoons were spent finishing anything left over from the morning, getting the records up to date and washing down the lab equipment. This left plenty of time for gossip, reading magazines and watching the antics of the dumper drivers. We were rewarded one day by the sight of the Cisco Kid cutting one corner too many and finishing up with his truck in a settlement tank. "Cisco's in the s**t" went out the call and we all ran out. Sure enough, there was Cisco's huge dumper truck well down in the effluent with Cisco perched on its roof. So, we all rushed out and watched the sport as a rather malodorous Cisco and his truck were recovered. He was much better behaved after that.

One of the guys at the lab devised a fiendish practical joke against the two girls who worked at the lab. The toilets were all a bit old fashioned and their cisterns were the old thunder boxes mounted high up on the wall. He waited until both girls had gone home for the day and went into one of their cubicles armed with a short length of rubber hose. He proceeded to fix this underneath the ballcock in the cistern at the point where water came out to refill the cistern once the chain had been pulled. The other end of the hose was left hanging over the front of the cistern. Next day, one of the girls went to the loo and of course pulled the chain to flush. Almost immediately water started to pour down on her and she shrieked mightily. She knew exactly who had done in and came flying soggily out and proceeded to chase the culprit round the lab and outside flailing at him with a magazine. The rest of us were absolutely doubled up with laughter and the boss had to go into the cubicle to remove the offending piece of hose before the whole floor got flooded.

I mentioned earlier the Rivers Inspector, Arthur Dixon, and he was a regular customer of the labs. His job was to inspect rivers, streams and sewers to look for illegal dumping of substances. So, he was always taking samples and bringing them back to us for checking. If he found something suspicious, he would work his way backwards up the watercourse checking every stream and outfall until he'd got to where it was entering the stream. Then it was back up every sewer and drain, raising manhole covers and dipping for samples for us to analyse until he'd nailed the culprits at the works that were polluting, and he had them bang to rights with an unbreakable chain of evidence from our tests. There were many stories about Arthur and his terrier-like persistence but one that made us chuckle a lot was when he was observed in the bucket of a crane swinging slowly backwards and forwards over the settlement tanks with a strange piece of equipment in his hand.

"What are doing Arthur, and what's that piece of kit you've got?" someone called when one his swings brought him within earshot.

"It's a Geiger Counter" called Arthur. "Some prat who was fitted with a radio-active suppository has lost it down the karzi and I'm trying to find it!"

On another famous occasion, he was checking one of the hidden streams that pass through Manchester city centre when a cook in restaurant above opened a window and dropped a load of kitchen scraps out straight onto Arthur's head. Arthur in his waders and oilskins, dripping with all sorts of peelings and waste, marched straight in to hotel reception of one of the poshest hotels in Manchester and demanded to see Manager for a bawling out before he got served with an infringement notice.

Only Arthur!

While I was working at Davyhulme, I became a regular reader of '*New Scientist*' and that was the end of my possible future career in science. Looking at the Situations Vacant, I found to my disbelief what a puny sort of salary I could expect to earn even after several years' experience and promotion. Because of my idleness, I'd ploughed my first year's exams at uni and was told that I'd have to resit. Looking at the job prospects decided me, and I declined the offer of a re-sit and carried on working at the labs for a few more months while I looked for something else.

Dad and Mum weren't too chuffed when I told them that I was not carrying on with my uni course and tried to persuade me to stay on and change to another course as I'd got very good results in classical subjects at O level. School hadn't been at all keen on me doing science in the sixth Form but had let me, and here it was looking like I'd made the wrong choice. By now, I wasn't thrilled at the idea of continuing in education having been through umpteen years of it and I was enjoying having a bit of cash in my pocket from my wages at the Lab. The bottom line was that I really had no idea what I wanted to do or what I'd be good at. It wasn't until some years later that I realised that I was very good at problem solving and therefore better suited to management.

Chapter Nineteen
Latter Days at the Farm

I managed to convince Dad and Mum that staying on at uni wasn't going to be in my best interests and I was probably helped by Bob who also hadn't known what he wanted to do, so he was now running the Farm with Dad. Dad was a keen Mason and therefore well connected with all sorts of other businessmen, so he made a few enquiries and came up with some suggestions. The one that I rather liked the sound of was banking. It sounded nice and clean after the sewage works. After making applications I was interviewed and offered a clerk's job at the Midland Bank who had a vacancy for a trainee at their Deansgate branch in the centre of Manchester. Even as a trainee bank clerk, the money was better than Davyhulme and the prospects were miles better. And a lot less smelly. I finished up working for the Midland for about five years until I got married.

I worked at Deansgate for best part of year then went to Southport for a couple of training courses at the Bank's school there where I and my fellow trainees had a riotous and dissolute time once classes had finished for the day.

After I been shown how to become a cashier, I got moved to Urmston as a back-room clerk and then a cashier proper working for a lovely Liverpudlian called George Carter. He was a mad keen supporter of Tranmere Rovers but then, nobody's perfect. My fellow cashier Pete Webster and I had a great time together and we were joined in our lunch-time and after hours drinking by our new assistant Manager, Jack Polkinghorn who was a hell of a nice guy. Jack was the most unlikely bank manager you have ever seen. He was huge, with a battered face and bent nose presumably from playing rugby but it could just as easily have been from prize fighting. Despite appearances he was a gentle soul and the customers liked him for his kindly ways. After almost two years at Urmston, George Carter was getting me ready to go on a course for the next leg up the ladder to become a Securities Clerk which was only one step below becoming an Assistant Manager.

But all good things come to an end and the summons came like a thunderbolt that I was to be transferred to Rusholme where they needed extra cashiers as they were expanding. It was no Securities Course for me. I tried protesting and was threatened with a posting to Ulverston, so I backed down very sharply. Rusholme wasn't too far from home so I could carry on living at the Farm. It turned out to be very busy and with a really first-class bunch of people running the counters of the 'home' branch at Rusholme (which is now at the beginning of Manchester's 'Curry Mile') plus sub-branches at Manchester University, Fallowfield and Upper Brook Street, all no more than a couple of miles away. It was seriously busy, and we all worked like demons, especially when closing down at the end of the business day when we had to add the figures for the day's transactions from the three sub-branches onto the main branch's figures to complete the day's accounts and then balance the books and the cash.

When not on the counter, I soon learnt to listen out for one of the cashiers greeting a customer with the phrase "Turned out nice again!" It was time to pop your head up from the rear of the bank and take a look, as this was code to tell us that an attractive woman had just come in. We were all a well-motivated and high-performing team, but the same group of staff had been around for quite a while. This was a bit unusual as Head Office liked to move experienced staff around to give a boost to branches that needed it or promote such staff and neither of these things had happened. Someone in HR spotted that lack of movement and then looked at the branch's performance figures and the branch manager's performance assessments of the staff. There was a clear discrepancy between the branch's excellent performance and the manager's low rating for individuals. He asked a Branch Inspector to pay us a visit and after a couple of days watching us at work, he was clear that we workers were being under rated by the Manager.

We heard that the Inspector reckoned that it was a deliberate ploy by the manager to keep the good staff that he'd got to make his life easier. Swine! The manager was disciplined and moved, and we all started to get promotions and moves.

One of the oddities of working at the sub-branches was that at Fallowfield and Upper Brook Street, you worked alone but were assigned a Guard for protection. Hah! Some protection! The Guards were all pensioners, so we reckoned that they were there to make sure we didn't run off with the cash! We used to pack a bag with as much cash in notes that we thought we'd need for the day then set off to the sub-branch _**on the bus**_ with the bag chained to our wrists containing between £3000 and £5000. How we didn't get mugged, I'll never know. Sanity eventually prevailed, and the bank coughed up for taxis to move us to and from. It was while I was working at the Upper Brook Street Sub-Branch that I spotted the TVR that I subsequently bought when it was on the forecourt of the garage opposite the branch. As mentioned earlier, this was fearsome beast as it had been very highly tuned, but it was a bit lairy in daily use because of its competition brakes. They just weren't that good unless you were stopping often from high speed, so it needed anticipation and care when driving in traffic. I sold it after a couple of years and bought a magnificent Bristol 405 Drop Head Coupe. It was ten years old but so well made and it was an absolute delight to drive. I did my courting in the Bristol and it carried over into my married life. I wish I still owned it because as well as having a lot of 'presence' and being great to drive, they're worth crazy money today.

My old Bristol 405 Drop Head Coupe photographed a few years ago. Only about forty of these cars were ever built

I was still helping out a bit around the Farm but not as much as before because the grains were now being delivered by tipper trucks it was so much easier to keep up with the flow from Kellogg's. I was now being paid fairly well by the bank, had a good group of friends at work and had a very good social life with a group of friends, many of them from my primary schooldays and I'd even joined the Young Conservatives! Not too surprising with both Dad and Mum being in politics and I'd met up with quite a few of them during election campaigns and fund raising and liked them. It was three of these lunatics who joined me in that crazy project to go to Italy in the old Daimler that subsequently blew up. I'm still in touch with two of them.

The main group that contained my friends from Primary School used to play Golf every week at Chorlton Golf Club plus snooker and cards in the evenings. I was also chasing round the pubs of Cheshire on one or two nights a week and there was usually a party to be found somewhere. The Golf Club group were my closest friends and steadily, they all got engaged and then married and we still knocked around as an enlarged group. So, it was only a matter of time before I joined the 'Just Married' club. I met my wife-to-be not through the

Golf Club group but through one of my Young Conservative mates. Frank had got engaged to Jane and I met Vicky at their engagement party as she was a friend of Jane. I thought Vicky was stunning and very bright, but I didn't make a great impression on her.

Jane said to her "Francis met you at the party and would like to go out with you."

Vicky said, "Which one was he?"

My wounded pride decided that it was not due to my lack of charisma but because she was busy dashing round serving snacks and drinks. Fortunately, although she couldn't remember a lot about me from the party, she agreed to go on a double date with me that was set up by Frank and Jane.

The rest, as they say, is history.

The three brothers, Francis, Bob and Oliver with their wives
Vicky, Nan and Alicia